DigitalFirst
Leadership

Master Social Media
Build Online Presence
Lead Your Tribe

RICHARD BLISS

BLISSPOINT PRESS

CONTENTS

For Stephanie

FOREWORD

Lying in a hospital bed in Hong Kong with a temperature of 104°F and a fever that was sending me into the cosmos, I tried to understand what the doctor was saying. He had just arrived with a big bag of needles and an even bigger bag of pills. "There are many strains of flu in Asia right now that are very dangerous," he told me. "If you were my son, I would tell you to take every needle and to swallow every pill." My head went reeling. Before I had the chance to ask any questions, he told me to swallow the fistful of meds he'd just put in front of me. Then he said, "*If* you wake up, I'll be here." *If*! With a spinning head and no other options, I gobbled down the pills and hoped for the best. It would be hard to describe how I felt the next twenty minutes before I passed out.

Hours later, I came to, dazed and drenched in cold sweat. The doctor sat at the edge of the bed. He just smiled and said, "I'm very happy you woke up." So was I. Just a few hours earlier, I was on my way home from one of many trips I had made that month, adding to the thousands of miles I would travel and thousands of people I would speak to that year alone. For decades, that was just how I lived. As the vice-chairman and former President of a major multi-billion-dollar tech firm, I was expected to make appearances, meet clients, give talks—and I loved it. There was nothing better than meeting face to face with customers and potential customers, listening to their needs and discussing how we could work together; or presenting to a crowd of eager faces and sharing knowledge that I knew could help them. I also had one of the best teams in the world behind me.

But when I ended up in that Hong Kongese hospital, I was burnt out. Not only had I fallen sick, but travel was taking its toll. Worse yet, I felt like I couldn't stop working, because even though I was reaching so many people, it never felt like it was enough. Making direct connections—whether working with colleagues, meeting clients' needs, or leading teams—are the heart of any company worth its salt, so not only did I want to connect with a wider audience, but I also wanted to engage directly with members of that audience in meaningful ways. This was something one couldn't always do when speaking to a crowd of one, two, five, or ten thousand.

It was about that time when I met Richard Bliss, and let me just say, he changed my life. I know this sounds dramatic, but after meeting Richard, I never again ended up splayed out on a hospital bed in East Asia, uncertain if the next time I closed my eyes I'd be taking the long dirt nap.

Before I met Richard, I had been skeptical—to say the least—of social media. I didn't understand its importance or see how it would benefit my clients, colleagues, or employees. It just seemed like a bunch of fluff. Not to mention, it was intimidating. What would I even talk about? Who would listen? But I also saw the writing on the wall—the world was changing. If I was going to maintain my role as a leader, I needed to change with it. Richard helped me realize this fact, and this is when I started getting serious about social media and online social conversations and connections. The results were bigger and better than I could've ever imagined.

Though I had some fun on Twitter, LinkedIn opened my eyes to the possibilities of connecting with my audience on a deeper level. Together, Richard and I created a number of videos, articles, and posts on a variety of topics. Some were prescriptive, while others delved into my opinions and stories I wanted to share. Getting them online and in front of people changed how I did business. I showed up in Chicago at a meeting with a large energy company, and they told me they were using my videos in training sessions with new employees—suffice to say, we signed a deal that day. When I gave talks, there would be people waiting before and after to tell me they'd come to see me specifically because of content I put up online. I started developing relationships with employees and customers that I would've never been able to even connect with if it weren't for the capabilities that social media provided. I also stopped logging so many frequent flyer miles.

Though Richard assisted me with the basics of setting up my profiles and showed me how these tools worked—and they were tools indeed—he was invaluable in helping me identify what I wanted to talk about online, what I wanted to be known for, and how my efforts would affect the company I helped run and the people I led. I always thought I was pretty damn good at my job, but Richard was a true coach when it came to social media, providing advice and support I hadn't known I needed. And come on, even Tiger Woods had a coach.

The lessons I learned from Richard are covered throughout this book—there are even some he hasn't yet taught me. Not only does he simplify the world of social media and how leaders can use it to their advantage, but he does so in a way that actually gets you excited about getting involved. There are few better feelings than having someone directly thank you for the insights you've provided or the stories you've shared; things that have actually helped people do their jobs, succeed in their roles, or that simply spoke to them on a personal level. In turn, you'll find how much their responses will mean to you.

Though I have retired from NetApp, and focus on board work today, the videos Richard and I made together, and popularized online through LinkedIn and other social media channels, are still used by companies and a number of universities (including my Alma Mater, Notre Dame). I am so honored to have the chance to share my knowledge with a younger generation, the future leaders of the world. Social media is by no means a question of ego or legacy (what I had wrongly assumed it was—Richard explains that it isn't), but a question of making a direct impact, helping people, making others feel valued and appreciated, and creating long-lasting, meaningful connections.

With Richard's guidance, you can do all of this and more, and when you do, it will change your life, too.

—Tom Mendoza,
former President and Vice-Chairman of
NetApp, 2021

DIGITAL-FIRST LEADERS IN A POST-PANDEMIC WORLD

DESPITE ALL THE ways for people to connect today, many of us remain disconnected. The technological capabilities spurred by the internet promised a new world of communication and commerce, and overall, they have delivered. Still, something seems to have been lost in translation. Sure, we're online—connected to our phones, computers, devices—but that doesn't necessarily mean we're connected with one another. We increasingly use the internet for all sorts of daily interactions and chores, whether scrolling our feeds, buying groceries, or paying our bills, but it's not so clear if the internet has brought us closer as individuals, groups, communities, or tribes. If it hasn't, then what's the point of it? And are there those among us who can use digital tools to bring us together and close this connection gap?

This sense of disconnection comes as no surprise. As a country and as a world, we have been through a lot lately, especially starting in 2020. The word "unprecedented" was thrown around a lot that year—and rightfully so. During those twelve months we experienced a pandemic; a global economic crisis; the worst unemployment rates in the US since the Great Depression;[1] an all-time high stock market;[2] shuttered shops, museums, music venues, and restaurants; potentially the largest protest movement the US has ever seen;[3] rabid bipartisanship and a contentious—to say the least—US presidential election; devastating wildfires across the western US; remote schooling; a reckoning of healthcare and childcare; a reframed understanding of what it means to be "essential"; and in general, a new approach to how we live our lives every single day.

Did I forget anything? Ah yes: work.

For many of us, how we work has changed forever. "Work-from-home" went from a nice-to-have employee perk to an absolute must, with kitchen-tables-turned-workspaces and commute times diminishing from minutes or hours to mere seconds. In-person sales pitches, keynotes, and conferences migrated to Zoom. There could be no more pounding the pavement or pressing palms, and no more deals were made over lunch or dinner. Instead, we had virtual job fairs, virtual hires, virtual onboarding, and virtual meetings: an all-encompassing virtual work experience.

The world at the beginning of 2020 looked a lot different than it did at the end when this book was being finished, and who knows what it will look like once the book is published. But the truth is,

---

1 Heather Long and Andrew Van Dam, "U.S. unemployment rate soars to 14.7 percent, the worst since the Depression era," *Washington Post*, May 8, 2020, https://www.washingtonpost.com/business/2020/05/08/april-2020-jobs-report/.

2 Investopedia Staff, "What Is the Dow Jones Industrial Average (DIJA) All-Time High?" *Investopedia*, April 12, 2020, https://www.investopedia.com/ask/answers/100214/what-dow-jones-industrial-average-djia-alltime-high.asp

3 Larry Buchanan, Quoctrung Bui, and Jugal K. Paterl, "Black Lives Matter May Be the Largest Movement in U.S. History," *New York Times*, July 3, 2020, https://www.nytimes.com/interactive/2020/07/03/us/george-floyd-protests-crowd-size.html

we were already headed in this direction of change and transformation to a more virtual world. Since the beginning of the century, technology has been flattening the world, shaping how we conduct commerce and communicate.[4] We can buy goods and services from anyone, anytime, anywhere—and sell products and services to anyone, anytime, anywhere—no matter our physical location. Even the smallest of companies can operate internationally, with employees from countries near and far and CEOs never having to leave their home offices if they so choose.

Traditional media has been forever altered by the internet; gone are the sales approaches of yore, when one-way advertising through magazines, newspapers, and television provided the most bang for our influence buck. Press releases and carefully prepared quotes, "big splash" announcements at annual events, and prepackaged narratives from corporate marketing departments have been lost to the lightning-speed exchange of information, the 24/7 news cycle, and all the digital noise that makes up the online world. Honest, regular engagement, not occasional empty messaging, has become paramount to breaking through to our audience, especially in times of crisis and immense change.

There is no doubt that such are the times we live in, and if the first two decades of this millennium were any indication, we will continue to live in similar conditions for many years to come. Social injustice, climate change, fear of economic failure, political division, the uncertain effects of automation, IoT, AI—many of these issues were already of concern before Covid-19 laid them bare, and no matter how hard we try, they're not going anywhere anytime soon. Of course, these issues do not exist in a vacuum either; they

---

4 Thomas L. Friedman, "It's a Flat World, After All," *New York Times* magazine, April 3, 2005, https://www.nytimes.com/2005/04/03/magazine/its-a-flat-world-after-all.html

directly impact how organizations function, how industries change and progress, and how businesses thrive or disappear into the ether.

A globalized, technology-based economy, a new media landscape, and sociopolitical shifts are issues that will ring throughout our lifetimes. And as business leaders—whether executives, managers, consultants, or entrepreneurs—we need to adjust to these realities, and we need to be part of the conversations about them. This allows us to better connect with our colleagues, lead our employees, engage our customers, and influence a greater sphere of stakeholders and shapeholders. Today, these conversations most often take place on social media platforms.

But we're not prepared. Many of us have yet to truly embrace social media as a way to build an audience, develop a tribe, and wield influence. As it stands, executives—the leaders that dominate the business world—are falling behind. According to the Connected Leadership Survey conducted by a global business advisory firm called the Brunswick Group, just 48 percent of the surveyed CEOs had social media accounts.[5] The most popular platform for this group was LinkedIn (44 percent of the respondents had an account).[6] These numbers are dismal. And this lack of participation doesn't go unnoticed: the same survey found that, by a ratio of two to one, employees would prefer to work for CEOs who use social media than those who do not.[7]

Here's the problem: a CEO's inability to master twenty-first century communication tools calls into question their ability to lead a twenty-first century organization. Over 50 percent of CEOs haven't even taken the first step of *using* social media tools, let alone

---

5 Ivan De Luce, "10 top CEOs with the best social media presence, ranked," *Business Insider*, June 11, 2019, https://www.businessinsider.com/most-connected-ceos-on-social-media-platforms-2019-6.

6 Ivan De Luce, "10 top CEOs with the best social media presence, ranked."

7 Ivan De Luce, "10 top CEOs with the best social media presence, ranked."

mastering them. What does that say to our teams, clients, and customers? And what does that say about the future of our careers?

With social media, we can utilize our private channels to tell our corporate story as well as harness our personality and values as a means of championing our organization. When we use our authentic voice to create a digital presence and develop a platform, we prepare ourselves not just to respond to crises, but also to seize opportunities. In the meantime, many people's first (and only) impressions of us will be based on how we behave and engage online, how we present ourselves and interact with the greater environment. As such, interaction with our digital presence needs to come first, before our physical presence.

We must therefore take the time and put in the effort to learn the social media tools that will make us effective digital-first leaders, allowing us to extend our vision and voice, continuously engage with our customers and clients, lead our people, and create lasting results. There is no better way to do so than through the underappreciated power of LinkedIn. LinkedIn is arguably the pinnacle of social media, almost entirely unscathed by the toxic sludge, bots, and ad-based revenue structures that have undermined our faith in so many social media platforms. As author Scott Galloway points out in *Post Corona: From Crisis to Opportunity*, only around 20 percent of LinkedIn revenues come from advertising.[8] The other 80 percent comes from LinkedIn Premium, LinkedIn subscriptions, and corporate accounts. Galloway states, "LinkedIn is the social media platform we're all hoping Facebook and Twitter would become."[9] And he's right. Though so often misconstrued as an online résumé,

---

8 Scott Galloway, *Post Corona: From Crisis to Opportunity* (New York: Portfolio, 2020), 36.
9 Scott Galloway, *Post Corona*, 37.

LinkedIn has become the center of our digital identity as we look to connect in a disconnected world.

NOT SOCIAL FOR SOCIAL'S SAKE

Executives and other business leaders' lack of social media participation is in part due to a continued misunderstanding of its purpose and how to use the major platforms, including Facebook, Twitter, Instagram, and LinkedIn. It begs the question: What even is social media in today's context and in the context of Digital-First Leadership?

Social media is more than absentmindedly posting personal updates on Facebook, political quips on Twitter, vacation photos on Instagram, or a new job promotion on LinkedIn. Social media is the use of modern online digital communication tools to engage with our audience, organization, and followers, whether this is through LinkedIn or Facebook, YouTube videos or podcasts, TikTok or blog posts. By doing so, we are able to grow our professional brand identity and, in the end, sell products and services to the people who need them the most.

While social media is the creation of content and sharing it online, it is part of our digital presence, which is a constant. Social media is the action, whereas digital—or online—presence is our overall involvement, what people find when they go Google us online. By sharing our insights, stories, and ideas through an easily accessible online medium, these nuggets of information meet our audience members—from fanatical followers to potential customers, and from seasoned veteran colleagues to college interns—wherever they are. These actions help grow our digital presence.

Contemporary leaders are now expected to have a strong position on many of today's pressing social issues, setting an example online first (and continuously), so their employees can draw from their actions, and their customers can directly engage with them. While the listening audience has completely moved online, executives and other leaders have been slow to follow. There is therefore an immediate need to get up to speed, so the world's business leaders can be heard and seen. Those leaders who get in front of the audience today have first-mover advantage and will be able to influence conversations going forward. If you choose to be one of them now, you'll still have a head start over the majority of leaders out there.

This book will guide you in the process towards digital-first leadership. It will focus on taking known leadership lessons and identifying how to transfer them to the online world. The following chapters detail specific principles leaders must understand and the steps they must follow to accelerate their mastery of the social media communication tools used today. Though the book focuses on LinkedIn, the lessons are applicable to most social media platforms, and specific suggestions for other platforms are included as well.

For many leaders who are new to social media, this may all sound overwhelming and intimidating. How should we share material and content? What should we share and why? Does it really work? Is it all worth it? It's not easy to overcome these concerns, and if alone it can be nearly impossible. Without someone there to assist us, we can become paralyzed by our own uncertainty; but with the help of someone with the right experience, someone we can trust, we can push through our fears and start using social media effectively, building our digital presence and leading through social media.

And I'm here to help.

WHO I AM AND WHERE I'M TAKING YOU

As a LinkedIn Top Voices Influencer and experienced executive communications manager and social media coach, I work with leaders of all kinds—from middle managers to Fortune 500 executives—to help them become more comfortable with social media and more fluent in social conversations, building both their platforms and confidence to best reach their audience. By helping them define their brand vision and strategies and develop high-caliber sales teams, their companies are then able to drive demand, generate new revenue, and increase brand awareness. In addition to working with businesses and organizations here in the US, I've consulted startups and high-growth technology companies in European, Middle Eastern, African, Asian Pacific, and Latin American countries, focusing on the global market while leveraging local diversity.

Prior to my current career, I was myself an executive vice president of marketing for a number of tech-related companies. This is where my curiosity and passion for developing a digital-first leadership persona comes from: I know first-hand how hard it can be to lead people, but I also recognize how social media doesn't only assist in leading others, but can also alter the entire way executives run companies and do business overall.

I've been on LinkedIn since 2006, but for a long time, my account there was idle, simply acting as a résumé holder and a place to keep track of people I worked with. Then something changed— the founder of the start-up I worked for at the time suddenly let me go. On top of that, the company gave that job to my wife (now ex-wife)… talk about awkward. I was in a position I had never imagined. Though I was well-known in my industry, had travelled the globe speaking at conferences, and worked closely with partners and customers, my social media presences was limited, and I began to see how much it was starting to hurt me.

I had been somewhat of a dabbler in social media early on, using it for more superficial purposes—in addition to being on LinkedIn within its first three years of existence, I started using Twitter within its first year. But it wasn't until I took the time to explore the platforms in detail that I realized the power of these tools. I decided I needed to reinvent myself, extend my voice, and build a new brand. First, I wrote a book on the business lessons I had learned as a vice president of marketing for more than eighteen years. Then, I set about teaching myself new skills. In addition to using the typical social media platforms, I also started a highly successful podcast called *Funding the Dream*, which became the leading voice in the space I was covering at that time. The podcast provided me with ways to meet people I wouldn't have normally met and further learn about the digital communication and leadership tools employed by the rising generation of workers.

When it came to LinkedIn, it quickly became obvious that it was much more than a place to record my work experience. It wasn't just a place to demonstrate my skills, but actually *do my work*. As a consultant, I began helping executives and business leaders all over the world realize this fact: LinkedIn is where you *do your work*. It's where you lead your team, influence your industry, connect with others, and deliver your vision.

Since then, I have spoken with hundreds of business and sales leaders about their use of social media, sometimes in person and many times virtually. And just like everyone else, when the pandemic hit, I had to adjust to an even newer set of realities. My backyard became my office (a tent workspace, complete with a desktop computer, green screen, and A/C), and I continued speaking, consulting, and working, but now entirely virtually.

From my own experience, research, and countless conversations over the years, I developed the principles and lessons I share throughout these pages. Though none of them are particularly difficult to grasp, they can often be difficult to put into practice, especially if you've been hesitant—or flat out resistant—to embracing social media as more than just a way to share photos of your family and keep up with your old college buddies. That's one of the reasons LinkedIn is the best platform to get you started. It's a professional tool where you don't just passively consume, but actively engage.

Together, we'll walk through each one of these principles and the actions to put them into practice, helping you get over any social media fears and insecurities, develop an authentic voice, and connect with others online. In doing so, you'll discover how to set yourself apart from other leaders out there today, design a strategic vision with your team, and create a true digital-first culture. You'll learn how to use the tools you need to succeed today, how to share (but not overshare) the right information and effective narratives with authority and power, and how to establish yourself as a true twenty-first century digital-first leader.

CHAPTER 1

FORGET WHAT YOU KNOW ABOUT SOCIAL MEDIA

"I DON'T CARE what the Kardashians had for breakfast."

When Tom Mendoza was asked about social media, this response was not surprising. As vice-chairman and former president of the six-billion-dollar hybrid cloud data services and data management company, NetApp, and for whom Notre Dame's Mendoza College of Business is named, Tom is what you might call old school. After working for a variety of tech firms in the 1980s, he joined NetApp as its thirty-second employee in 1994 (as of 2020, the company had over 10,000 employees). For his first twenty years at NetApp, Tom never travelled less than 250,000 miles, crisscrossing the globe to meet with customers, partners, and prospects—all without a personal computer.

Then, in 2012, Tom had something of an epiphany. On a flight home from Mumbai, where he had just given presentations to 10,000 people over two days, including India's top IT leaders, NetApp employees in Bangalore, and CEOs of some of the largest companies in the country, he reflected on the stories he had shared. Overall, he was proud of what he had done, feeling he had connected with and made an impact on the members of his audience, who showed their appreciation through thundering applause and resounding praise. But as he sat on the plane, something nagged at him: though 10,000 people was far from insignificant, there were over 1.3 billion people in India—he'd only really spoken to a tiny sliver of them. Even if he kept travelling around the world for the rest of his career, speaking to group after group, he could only ever reach a mere fraction of all the people he hoped to reach.

Tom wanted to amplify his voice, increase his reach, and connect not just with 10,000, but tens of thousands, hundreds of thousands—millions even! And though he was loath to admit it, he started to think that social media, which he had previously seen as nothing more than a cesspool of vanity and mindless entertainment, could help him get there.

When he landed stateside, after an unfortunate stopover in Hong Kong as recounted in the Foreword, he spoke with his team and they got to work. Though still hesitant, YouTube seemed like a natural place for him to ease into social media. He was already comfortable delivering speeches and he was (and remains) a gifted speaker, so he thought all his team had to do was put him in front of a camera and press record. Together, they created a dozen short videos, each about three minutes long, based on the successful talks he had given around the globe. These videos were then posted to NetApp's corporate YouTube channel.

Though an admirable effort, these videos received little attention in the beginning. Tom's audience was not used to looking on the company website or YouTube channel to find what he had to say. Like him, people were accustomed to his in-person, on-stage talks. Or they'd heard from him from time to time through individual, direct emails or an occasional press release issued by the NetApp PR team. While he had an audience, he still didn't have an *online* audience, so directing traffic to the videos was off to a sluggish start.

He asked his team what they should do next?

Some members seemed confused by the question. In their minds, there was no "next." The videos had been created and posted online—end of story. But that wasn't enough for Tom. He wasn't looking to just get his message online; he was looking to get his message in front of people who could *benefit* from it. He knew that wasn't going to happen overnight, but he also realized he needed to take part in social media on a much deeper level. To that end, he began making more YouTube videos on a wider array of topics.

In these videos, he spoke about issues he'd never previously discussed, but they were ones he could talk about on a rolling basis as they came up, developing ongoing conversations, instead of one-way messages. From there, he had help transcribing these videos and reworking them into publishable articles. He was sharing the same content as before, but through *Forbes.com* and other outlets, he started gaining a wider following. If he had something to say on leadership, he shared it; if he had thoughts on public speaking, he wrote about them. He wasn't constrained by the business limits of subject matter. He had a plethora of useful material from public speaking to draw upon. Tom's content was not tied to an event, date, or time. It was evergreen.

As such, Tom was developing his own voice online, and it was resonating with a new audience. But he needed to find a means of engaging more directly with his audience. He needed to get beyond the limits of NetApp's corporate social media accounts and develop his own. That's when he started a LinkedIn account.

For Tom, and many executives like him, LinkedIn was still perceived as a job board, so he was hesitant, not seeing the necessity or urgency to use a platform that was solely for "finding a job." He also worried he'd get swamped with messages from people looking for jobs or otherwise wasting his time. He wondered why he would want to put himself in that situation (he'd later find that this was a nonissue). But Tom was willing to move beyond his concerns, to step out and experiment.

After setting up his account, he began resharing the same YouTube videos he had previously posted on his company's channel, but now on his LinkedIn profile. Though there was limited interest in the videos on the corporate YouTube channel, he now found that his growing number of LinkedIn connections were pining after them. The videos reached an audience who had never watched Tom deliver a speech. In addition, he was able to go back to his *Forbes* articles and repost them to LinkedIn, further opening up this content to his new audience. And for those who had watched or read his speeches in the past, LinkedIn gave them the ability to share these with their own networks easily, increasing Tom's message and boosting his brand. He also started a Twitter account to develop another wide-reaching platform. His digital presence was revving up.

Tom was in no hurry. He was willing to grow his network organically, regularly creating and sharing material, slowly building a following that came to anticipate, and then amplify, his content. In addition, Tom mastered the use of LinkedIn on his mobile devices. He posted, commented, shared, and liked on a regular basis. These actions became so ingrained in his daily routine that at one point he was asked in a comment if he hired someone in the background to write and post all this material for him, or if it was really him.

"Of course, it's me," he responded, "Who else would it be?"

In just a few years, Tom could put out a post on his LinkedIn profile that generated more than 300,000 views from around the world, reaching more people than in all his years of traveling and speaking. When he retired in 2019, after twenty-five years with the company, Tom didn't make the announcement with a press release. He didn't do it with a speech or even an internal email to his colleagues and employees. Instead, he crafted a short message and posted it to his LinkedIn and Twitter accounts. In less than twenty-four hours, more than 140,000 people had read his posts. Of them, 600 left comments and thousands clicked the like button, showing their support. And then using his smartphone (to this day, he still hasn't bought a personal computer), Tom responded to each of those 600 comments, expressing his gratitude and appreciation for their words. Hundreds of thousands of people ended up reading and sharing his retirement announcement, and if they made a comment, they knew Tom was the one on the other end taking the time to tap out a thoughtful response.

Tom's early hesitance to social media came from a mix of misconstruing its purpose today and, as he would likely admit, from good old-fashioned fear, instilled by the pervasive myths surrounding these communication tools. Like many leaders, he fell into the trap of thinking social media is just a toxic wasteland of celebrity selfies, direct marketing, partisan bickering, and misinformation. Though there's some truth there, by entirely writing off social media we miss out on an opportunity that can revolutionize the way we lead. With better understanding of how social media can connect us with our targeted audience, our fear of these online communication and leadership tools tends to subside. By putting many of the social media myths to bed, even the most skeptical can harness these tools' full power, provide value for their audience, and feel rewarded in return.

INFLUENCE, NOT CONSUMPTION

The in-person keynote as we know it may be dead. Large conferences are unlikely to make a comeback anytime soon, and auditorium-style company-wide meetings could be a relic of the past. It's tough. As leaders, many of us are used to these talks and gatherings. They're where we feel comfortable, and they give us an opportunity to shine, thrive, and inspire, all in real time. This approach is still favored by a particular demographic of leaders—a somewhat older, traditional generation—but due to the available technology and unavoidable circumstances, this in-person concept, and the resulting culture, is changing. It's no longer about getting butts in seats.

Take any member of the same leadership group and ask them if they would take you up on the following: putting them in front of 6,000 of their most ardent fans and customers, with the ability to talk about anything they want, and the opportunity to interact directly with their audience. Most would say "absolutely" and jump at this offer. What they don't often see however, just like Tom Mendoza didn't see at first, is that today, that's what LinkedIn does, that's what Twitter does, and that's the power of social media.

Still, many of us scrutinize social media, seeing it at its worst: politicians trading barbs and pop stars focused on personal daily minutiae. We see our children, and in some cases our grandchildren, totally obsessed. What are they staring at? What are they banging out with their thumbs at a hundred miles per hour? To the casual, uninitiated observers, social media can look a lot like watching the TV shows of our youth, plopping down, our faces inches from the screen, and drooling over *Gilligan's Island* or *I Dream of Jeannie*. Basically, many of us just don't get it.

Even if we recognize social media as a set of powerful communication and leadership tools, many of us lump it in with other marketing devices. There is a misconception that the social media approach is no different from the classic bullhorn approach: a company pushes content out, blasting it to everyone who might see, hear, or read it. As discussed in the Introduction, in the past, this took place through traditional broadcasting mediums, like running a single ad on television, on the radio, or in a magazine.

This concept is referred to as "interrupt marketing." The idea is to generate content for a captured audience who will pay attention to the ad since it's interrupting something it wants to see, hear, or read, and this audience has to get through the ad to do so. Interrupt marketing is a one-way, one-to-many tool, indiscriminate and impersonal technique. This age-old approach has become a mindset, which has created mental blocks to fully understanding how we can engage with our audience through social media.

We no longer have a captive mass audience with no choice but to lock into the content we're pushing. Media, news, and information in general are both widely distributed and fragmented, meaning individuals now pick and choose what content they consume and where, when, and how they consume it. This fact requires us to make fundamental changes to our mindsets and to the way we deliver information to our buying audience. We have to cut through a tsunami of distractions to reach people, and even then, we have to capture their attention long enough to help them realize we have a product or service they want or need, even if they didn't realize it before. Social media allows us not just to speak to this audience directly, but to actually interact with it, discovering its interests and helping it find solutions to its problems. We can't do this, however, if we don't go out of our own way.

THE THREE MYTHS: TIME, SELF-PROMOTION, AND RELEVANCE

By realizing social media is not simply consumption, but a way for leaders to inspire and influence others, it's possible to learn how to use these tools more effectively. Sure, you can sit around and watch videos through the "Hold My Beer" Twitter handle until your eyes bleed (I don't recommend it), but that's not the point. As discussed, social media is *not* just entertainment: it provides the ability to lead, influence, inspire, and guide others. You must therefore reframe your understanding of social media and the power it has for you, your career, and your organization. The best place to start is by dispelling the most common social media myths holding you back. There are three in particular that you need to overcome before you can move forward.

MYTH #1: WHO'S GOT THE TIME? NOT ME!

One of the biggest challenges for any leaders new to social media is bandwidth. We have to find the time to post, read, and respond to others, dedicating a significant amount of our day (which we may believe could be better spent elsewhere). Many of us are also concerned about people we barely know (or don't know at all) making inappropriate claims on our attention and time, pestering us about jobs, connections, or other favors. The reason this myth remains so strong is because few of us habitually use social media in the context of work. In order for it to become a habit, we have to disrupt our normal routine to insert a new one that includes skills that may feel foreign to us. Not only do we have to come up with content, but we need to learn how to post and share what we want to say.

On top of this, the early, immediate rewards of social media are limited. Having ten, or even a hundred, Twitter followers won't motivate anyone toward an action. Compared to other accounts with thousands, a small one is unlikely to push the needle. These early stages make it hard for us to break out of our traditional behaviors and adopt social media on a deeper level. The positive reinforcement feedback loop is out of alignment, leading to exasperation—what's the point of putting in all this time and effort if no one is listening? But social media doesn't need to take up nearly as much of our day as we might expect, and eventually, our audience will inevitably grow.

You can start modestly, dedicating seven minutes a weekday to building your digital presence. When you break it down, that's just a little over thirty minutes a workweek, or two hours a month. That's all it takes. In those seven minutes, share an idea or a thought about a topic of discussion on the platform you're using. Throw out a small nugget of wisdom, a snippet of your day, or an anecdote of significance. Such "tiny little engagements" begin to establish your presence and allow your voice to be heard. Start with fifty words. Then next week, come up with fifty more. Your content and advice don't have to be perfect in these early stages either, just good enough.

Don't try to be edgy, controversial, or act as if you're handing down some kind of earth-shattering advice from the heavens above—simply be yourself and give your honest opinion, making short posts and commenting on others' content. Using this "seven-minute rule," you'll start forming a habit, and these tiny little engagements will become larger. As you begin seeing results, you'll find that you want to, and are able to, go beyond those seven minutes. Though there is not enough time in the world to consume all the information streams you are subjected to each day, by being part of the conversations ricocheting across the online atmosphere, you'll have taken the first step in making a lasting impact in how you communicate and lead—and it won't take up much of your time.

MYTH #2: JUST A BUNCH OF SELF-PROMOTION

Leaders often conflate social media with self-promotion. Yes, some social media participants make it all about themselves—the TikTok stars, the Kardashians of the world, the Instafamous out for that perfect selfie—and that's likely to scare many of us off. Why? Because as leaders, and executives in particular, we've been trained to draw attention to the company, corporation, or brand, not ourselves. We've been taught that when it comes to the public face of the organization, we need to follow the corporate lead. We're used to PR and marketing teams carefully crafting and editing what we say, choosing what message we should send out into the atmosphere, leaving us with little personal agency. Since that's the case, many of us have avoided uncensored, organic conversations with our customers or clients, the types of conversations in which we would pull in our personal beliefs, thoughts, and narratives, because doing so would feel too much like self-promotion.

But social media thrives on these types of conversations. Previously, PR and one-way marketing acted as a gatekeeper between leaders and their followers, but in this hyper-connected, online environment, those gates have been torn down, not for our own self-promotion, but so we can provide our audience with value directly. When we are able to interact with our audience, we can better understand what it really wants. The focus here shouldn't be on a specific deliverable, either—it needs to be wider and more foundational than mere products. We want to discover our audience's desired emotional state. Do these people want to be happy? Satisfied? Excited or entertained? Are they lonely and seeking inclusion? Are they angry and seeking justification? When we develop a digital presence that breaks down the wall between us and our customers, we can begin to truly answer these questions, understanding the complexities of what they're looking for—something that can't be easily translated into a thirty second radio spot or banner ad.

Keep in mind, "audience" does not just refer to consumers, customers, and clients, but also our own colleagues and teams. They, too, want to hear directly from us. They want to understand where we're coming from, what we believe in, what we have to teach them, and how we can help them—in short, where we're leading them. Previously, much of that could have been done in the office. Our visibility came from our physical presence in the cafeteria, boardroom, team meetings, and hallways, and it gave us a chance to connect. Now, with global operations and with so many of us increasingly working from home, this opportunity is lost. Our physical presence has been replaced with our digital presence; our in-person dialogues have been transferred online.

By engaging your audience, you give it the value it's looking for. When you take the time to connect with people and understand what they want or need, you can then provide necessary solutions. As a leader, your role is to know what your customers, colleagues, and employees are looking for, and why they think you can give it to them. This situation requires a shift in your thinking about what it means to lead. True leadership is all about serving those whom we lead; the focus shouldn't be on ourselves, it should be on our audience. This means self-promotion for self-promotion's sake is the antithesis of true leadership, and it has no place in social media for digital-first leaders.

MYTH #3: NOTHING RELEVANT TO SAY

With social media, the opportunities for expanding conversations are unlimited, but the myth of having nothing relevant to say keeps leaders from making their voices heard. As social media now allows direct two-way conversations with our audiences, it can be a frightening new experience going off script and trusting our own internal voice. The added pressure of not knowing what to do or what to say can create anxiety that causes us to say nothing at all. But when we remain silent, we lose a major opportunity. The challenge is to mine our personal experiences and open up discussions that we may be surprised anyone's even interested in.

Take Peter McKay, for example, the current CEO of a major security software firm. Over the years, Peter has led a number of organizations, and whenever they exhibited at major conferences, he could often be found walking the trade show floor. He always made sure to visit his company's booth to say hello, make an appearance, and most importantly to him, check out the carpet... Yes, the carpet. Or more specifically, the padding underneath the carpet. In his early years in the industry, trade show after trade show, Peter was stuck on his feet running a booth all day. All that separated his shoes from the hard concrete floor was a thin layer of synthetic fibers. He vowed to himself that if he were ever in a position to fix this problem, he most certainly would. As a CEO, he made it a priority that, at every show, his company's booths have the thickest floor padding available, and he personally checks to make sure his instructions are followed.

Peter has been doing this for years, but it wasn't until he posted about it online that people took notice. He was so used to this trade show check, it had never occurred to him that it might be interesting to others outside of the people it directly affected. But in 2018, he began using social media more seriously, and he decided to create a small post about this simple action—it became one of his highest engagement posts with both his employees and customers. People could relate, and they understood the pain very well. They also were amazed that the leader of a billion-dollar company was so committed to his employees that he would test the trade show floor for thickly padded carpet, taking direct care of his team. This story spoke volumes about Peter's leadership.

In different times, a story like this would have been lost as a throwaway comment. But because it was captured as a social media post, it created an impact on thousands of people. Peter had no idea he would receive such a response—he didn't see how relevant this story was until he actually brought it to his audience. We all have something relevant to say, we just need to become aware of the material around us that can be useful and, like Peter, harness it for engagement.

The best way to get started in identifying relevant material is through a self-assessment. (Though there are many approaches to doing a self-assessment, one of the most effective is the Personal Branding framework from the Mercer-MacKay Digital Executive Program, which, with their permission, the following is based on.) This assessment should focus on what you've accomplished, and help you better understand the strengths you can bring to a conversation. Of course, like the carpet on the concrete floor, it's also important to pay attention to the little things. To begin, pick three words that best describe how you want to be seen by your audience, including your customers, partners, colleagues, employees, and the public. Think about what you want to be known for. Examples might include:

achiever	focused
adventurous	honest
ambitious	knowledgeable
appreciative	loyal
authentic	motivational
brave	optimistic
caring	organized
collaborative	purposeful
competent	respectful
confident	successful
contributor	supportive
courageous	teacher
dependable	team player
determined	trusted
effective	unique
energetic	versatile

Next, consider what you're passionate about. What do you stand for? What beliefs and values are core to who you are as a person and leader? A good way to develop some ideas is to consider if anything has happened recently that you feel a need to speak out about. If so, what, and why? This could be a major event that affected your industry or company in particular, or one that resonated on a wider social or cultural scale.

Based on these answers, fill out the following self-assessment statement:

In my professional life, I want to be known as a _____ leader, who helps my employees, colleagues, and partners achieve or become _____, and who provides _____ to my customers and consumers.

I want to make an impact on the larger public and greater world through _____. My biggest challenge to fulfilling these goals is _____. I can overcome these challenges and achieve these goals by engaging my audience through _____.

How you answer these questions and fill out the self-assessment statement will help you source the material you'd like to share online, including themes and topics that you want to be associated with. For example, if you want to be known for equality, fairness, or as a visionary, you can draw on content that reinforces these aspirations. With social media, you're also given a chance to show your human side, so don't hold back. You have to be willing to allow others to peek into your life a bit, to see that you, too, are facing challenges, and witness how you handle them. In this process, you're sharing your personal growth and developing a closeness with your audience—and what could be more relevant than that?

OVERCOMING FEAR THROUGH COMMITMENT

Even when we begin to understand the purpose and power of social media and recognize that the three myths are entirely false, we are often still paralyzed from taking action. We'll even rely on the myths as justification for this paralysis. Whether we're long-time CEOs or first-time team leaders, opening ourselves up to inspection and potential ridicule in front of thousands of people is terrifying. We don't want to look foolish or embarrass ourselves, as we're afraid it could hurt our careers, our brands, and our companies. On an even more basic level, we might be scared to admit that we have no idea what we're doing when it comes to social media, and asking for help just highlights our ignorance and undermines our authority.

Essentially, our insecurities get the best of us. We ask, what if we put ourselves out there and we're exposed as some type of fraud, undeserving of our success? Though to some this question may sound like an irrational fear, it typifies the imposter syndrome that can riddle people with self-doubt, causing them to question their self-worth and personal and professional achievements. These feelings are far from uncommon: nearly 70 percent of people experience impostor syndrome at one point or another in their lives, worried that they're still faking it, instead of ever really making it.[10]

In the meantime, many people in positions of authority or notoriety who "lead" through social media come across as totally clueless. They make posts that are embarrassing—full of misinformation, half-baked thoughts and ideas—and repost material they may have never fully read or watched, or that comes from questionable sources. Even if they're trying to make a valid argument or point, it can get lost in sloganeering, lies, and incoherence. Their egos take the wheel and off they go, making reckless comments to millions, unconcerned with the potentially dire results. Unfortunately, these leaders' actions are what reinforce our fear.

As a true leader, however, part of your job is to overcome this fear and join in the online conversations happening right now. Recognize that you're not alone; countless leaders are in your exact same position. They're the same ones that look around at the virtual world and think, "Hey, my kids know how to do this. My employees know how to do this. But when I go out to do this, I'm just going to flat out embarrass myself—maybe even lose some business in the process!" These thoughts are self-defeating and totally unnecessary. You must become comfortable with discomfort and check your pride and ego at the door. If you make a small mistake, it's not the end of

---

10 Jaruwan Sakulku, "The Impostor Phenomenon," *The Journal of Behavioral Science* 6 (1), 75–97, https://so06.tci-thaijo.org/index.php/IJBS/article/view/521.

the world—typos can always be edited. If you need to ask for help, you're not signaling a failure in knowledge but a success in seeking it.

And if you hesitate to incorporate social media into your leadership because you believe your missteps might reflect poorly on yourself, then you're ironically doing the exact opposite—not being engaged on social media *actually* reflects poorly on you! As stated in the Introduction, your inability to master modern twenty-first century communication tools calls into question your ability to lead a twenty-first century organization. By committing yourself to learning these tools and mastering the language of social media, you're committing yourself to leading, and in so doing, you will overcome your fears. You need to be willing to take a risk, accept the possibility of embarrassment, and humble yourself to step out. When you do, you'll find that you'll get back so much more than you ever put in.

GRATITUDE FOR VALUE

In 2012, singer-songwriter Amanda Palmer found herself in a bit of a predicament. Though she'd enjoyed a successful career in music over the past decade—first as a member of the Boston-based Dresden Dolls, a self-described "Brechtian punk cabaret"[11] duo, and then eventually as a solo artist—and enjoyed the accolades of a cult following, when she pitched a new album to a record label that year, she was promptly turned down. This pitch had been a big decision for Amanda—in the past, she had put out her music on her own and gave it away to her fans for free. Involving a label would change that dynamic, but she saw it as an opportunity to grow. This opportunity was of course cut short: the label believed there were probably only 25,000 fans worldwide who would be interested in this project, and

11 Julia McCoy, "Great Copywriting in Action: Creative Artist Amanda Palmer," ExpressWriters.com, July 30, 2014, https://expresswriters.com/great-copywriting-in-action-creative-artist-amanda-palmer/.

when they crunched the numbers, they decided it wasn't worth it for them to pursue.

Rather than give up, Amanda turned to Kickstarter, a relatively new crowdfunding platform at the time. She reached out to her fans, asking for their support. Over the years, she had certainly paid her indie-rock dues, grinding out show after show, starting out in small clubs, couch surfing on tour, meeting fans and crashing at their homes. She was dedicated to her art, committed to her fans, and it showed. So it was only natural that her fans would respond in kind. After putting her project on the platform, she received over $1,192,793—the most money ever raised at that point for a music category on Kickstarter.

And here's the clincher—she was backed by 24,883 fans. Apparently, the record label knew their market with almost laser precision. Yes, there were only about 25,000 people who would buy this music from Amanda, but what the label failed to understand was the power of a strong following to sustain an artist—a true fan base will be spurred into action, responding to someone they believe has given them something important, even priceless.

Amanda later shared her story in a moving TED talk in 2013.[12] During her presentation, she explained a very simple yet central idea to building a tribe and following: when you give your audience something of value, it wants to give back. If you provide it with a mechanism to do so, a way to say thank you, it whole-heartedly will. Amanda's fans thanked her for her art by paying for her music. After years of giving her music to them for free, they gave back over one million dollars.

Though some may argue that Amanda is by no means a quintessential business leader—she'd likely argue the same—this story

---

12 Amanda Palmer, "The Art of Asking," TED, YouTube.com, March 1, 2013, https://www.youtube.com/watch?v=xMj_P_6H69g.

exemplifies the willingness to engage our audience through today's mediums. It's unlikely she could've ever raised the money for her new album if it hadn't been for Kickstarter, which is another twenty-first century digital communication tool, and a form of social media. But it would've been impossible if she hadn't built a true connection with her following in the first place.

Today, we can build this type of connection from the comfort of our own homes, probably much more comfortable than crashing on someone's lumpy couch while on tour. If we get over the misunderstandings, myths, and fear of social media, we can give something of value to our audience. If we build up goodwill by providing this value, when the time comes, our audience members will want to give back to us. They may give back by buying our product or backing a charity we support, but no matter what they give, it will be something of themselves in return for what we have given them.

For many of us trained in the marketplace, transactions of value usually include an exchange of money for goods or services. The idea of a transaction taking place as an exchange of ideas for attention is therefore difficult to grasp (and one of the reasons Myth #2, Just a Bunch of Self-Promotion, is so entrenched in our thinking). A transaction of loyalty and belief in exchange for a person's inspiration almost sounds like a cult of personality. Most people are not comfortable with this concept—but it's not as bizarre or strange as it sounds. This principle is actually all about showing gratitude and giving thanks.

The keyword here is "giving"—giving something to your audience, your tribe. Sometimes you could be giving a helpful opinion or a worthy piece of advice. Sometimes you could be giving your vulnerability. You can give your time by volunteering, your expertise by sharing, your financial support by donating, your moral support by participating—or you can give through all these avenues. No matter what you give and how, think of it as giving a part of yourself, a way to show your humanity and engage with your audience on a deeper level. In response, it will recognize that you've placed something of value into a conversation or an idea—into the collective common that is open to everyone to learn from. Your audience will see that you've added value, and so when the time comes to make a big ask, it's much more willing to reply.

That big ask might be something of monetary value, but it might also be something like patience or understanding. If you've built goodwill with the audience, it'll allow you such considerations. Think of Tesla and all the problems they had early on, causing them to delay the release of vehicles. Their fans stuck by them, willing to wait for a vehicle that promised to revolutionize the industry and help build a greener future. They had been inspired by the goal of changing the world, and this vision alone provided them with value. They were buying into an idea that resonated with them as much as they were buying a physical product.

Most consumers and employees are used to being asked for something of value from a company's leaders *before* those leaders have actually provided value to them. For consumers, this is typically their money; for employees, this is typically their time and efforts. But when leaders make demands before they have actually given to others—to their network, community, or tribe—their intentions seem hollow. Social media is an opportunity to provide your voice, your ideas, and your opinions, all of which have value to your audience, while also proving you are personally invested in that community's success. These actions are all part of building communities, and as part of a community you must participate every single day. Like Amanda Palmer, you need to provide value to engage your audience members. Do so consistently, and they won't just be willing to give back, they'll *want* to give back.

CONCLUSION

Before we can properly use social media as the powerful twenty-first century communication and leadership tool that it is, we must first better understand its purpose and power. If we allow ourselves to fall into the archaic thinking of the one-way bullhorn approach to influencing others, we'll never fully grasp the importance of social media and how it can be used to directly engage with our audience—be they colleagues, employees, customers, or the public—and create two-way conversations. Though so many people on social media make it all about themselves, stroking our own ego and supporting our vanity is never the point. The point is to connect, and through these connections, lead.

Still, fear abounds. There are both personal concerns and persistent myths that keep us from participating in social media and building our digital presence, which only serves to hurt us in the long run. We must recognize these myths as simply false and force ourselves to get over our fears so we can become active in the many pertinent conversations happening online today. We must also provide value with every comment, post, or repost we make, giving to our audience and growing our community. And when we provide value to our audience for free, we can get so much back in return. We will have gained a community that will support our endeavors and answer "yes" when presented with our big ask.

CHAPTER 2

DEVELOP YOUR AUTHENTIC VOICE

AFTER 2018, PETER McKay—the carpet-conscious CEO introduced in Chapter 1—decided he needed a break. Feeling his life was somewhat out of balance, he left the company he was with at the time to refocus, gain some perspective, and plan his next move. Still, he had taken to social media over the past year, and he decided to stay active online—even though he wasn't actively leading a company—discussing the journey he was taking. Uncertain of his next professional move, he shared more about his personal life, including what led him to take his "gap year" from work. He also participated in a triathlon to raise money for a cancer charity in honor of his late mother. Due, in part, to his online connections, he was able to raise nearly $40,000 for the cause—the most of any individual competitor at the triathlon. His audience actually grew during that time, with thousands of people engaging with his content, even though it wasn't "business related." As Peter showed his true, authentic self, including his cares and concerns, it resonated with his audience like never before.

When he returned to the workforce in 2019, he was refreshed and energized. He also brought what he had learned about himself and about social media to his new job. Not only had he built a consistent flow, or cadence, of social conversations and posts, he had also done a bit of soul-searching—using a self-assessment similar to the one in Chapter 1—to help him identify what he wanted to be known for going forward. The main attribute was empathy, and he would quickly find in 2020 that this was a much-needed trait. As Covid-19 hit, and so many people began working from home, he realized that productivity was through the roof. Though most leaders would see this as a positive, Peter was concerned about the mental health of his employees.

They were already up against added pressures, fears, and isolation due to the pandemic, and now a lot of them were losing all sense of balance. Stuck at home, bored, and with little to do, they were working more than ever before, an entirely unintended consequence. Some just didn't know when to turn their screens off and call it a day. Peter remembered what it was like when his life was out of balance because of work, and he truly felt for his employees. He reached out to them through LinkedIn. Hoping to change their frame of reference, and speaking to them with honesty, authenticity, and care, he asked that they consider this time as an opportunity to focus on themselves and their personal lives, not just their jobs. Then he called for a company-wide global mental-health day. His words resonated with his followers, and they responded. Receiving 3,000 likes and 183 comments, the LinkedIn algorithm picked up on the high levels of engagement and amplified his post—170,000 LinkedIn users ended up seeing it.

When Peter shifted focus online to his personal journey and further built on his empathy for his employees, his followers grew. Based on his previous posts, current posts, online social conversations, and overall online presence, they believed his voice was credible and authentic. They were willing to follow the conversation where he was taking it because they trusted his authenticity, honesty, and leadership. With his audience in mind, Peter continued to make posts about a wide array of topics. They were often connected to his company's services and mission, but he would sometimes discuss issues and ideas that were important to him on a more personal level.

As a leader, Peter had a responsibility to his organization, and he couldn't use his position solely for a personal platform. But on occasion, he could use it to expound on something personal, an idea or thought that would likely continue to build a deeper connection with his audience and engage new followers. Like Peter, it's important to be cognizant of our roles as business leaders. We still have a responsibility to the health and success of the company we work for, and our followers only want to see our personal side when it feels appropriate. To build our brands and support our companies, we must therefore strike a balance, and it's impossible to do so without an authentic and believable voice.

Authenticity creates trust with the people we work with, sell to, and lead, and it allows us to speak our truth while inspiring others to do the same. We can use our voice to extend our personal brand online and participate in the conversations happening there, but we will only build a larger audience, tribe, and community, if people trust what we have to say. Trust in leaders doesn't always come easy, and with today's predominantly skeptical worldview, it can be hard won. We must therefore not just signal authenticity but actually *be* authentic. Our audience isn't stupid—it knows when we're putting on a show. Though we shouldn't force our opinions down anyone's throats, or overshare the private details of our personal lives, we also don't want people to think there's some emotionless bot on the other side of the screen running our social media accounts. Therefore, we need to recognize and support the reasons for which people will listen to us, believe in us, and follow us where we lead them.

AUTHENTICITY IN ACTION

The name "Bloomberg" is well-known, whether it refers to Bloomberg LP, the data, software, financial, and media company; Bloomberg Philanthropies, one of the largest US philanthropic organizations;[13] or the name Michael Bloomberg itself, the founder of both Bloomberg LP and Bloomberg Philanthropies, and the mayor of New York City from 2002 to 2013. Though Bloomberg's never been far from the public eye, he was front and center for a brief moment from mid-November to early March 2019, when he joined the already bloated race for the Democratic nominee for President of the United States. Still, just because his name was well-known in some circles, it didn't mean the entire country was all that familiar with the multi-billionaire executive, the once Republican, and former mayor.

He came out swinging on the national stage in TV ads and prepared statements online. "Defeating Donald Trump—and rebuilding America is the most urgent and important fight of our lives," he said, "and I'm going all in. I offer myself as a doer and a problem solver—not a talker. And someone who is ready to take on the tough fights—and win."[14] He also went big on spending, including 35 million dollars in television commercials within the first few days of his campaign to introduce, or reintroduce, himself and his political agenda to the masses.[15] At this point, he had outspent many of the advertising budgets of other primary Democratic campaigns.

Most importantly, his social media campaign was brilliant.

---

13 Pensions & Investments, "The Largest Foundations," pionline.com, November 12, 2018, https://www.pionline.com/article/20181112/ONLINE/181109876/the-largest-foundations.

14 Alexander Burns, "Michael Bloomberg Joins 2020 Democratic Field for President," *The New York Times*, November 24, 2019, https://www.nytimes.com/2019/11/24/us/politics/michael-bloomberg-2020-presidency.html.

15 Burns, "Michael Bloomberg Joins 2020 Democratic Field for President."

Though he'd spent a lot of money on those TV ads, he and his team recognized the need to get his message in front of a younger audience, who turned to social media for information and entertainment instead of television. When many younger people watch TV, they do so through a streaming service, entirely skipping the commercials and ads when possible. Recognizing this reality, he started pushing out his message via Facebook, Twitter, and Instagram. He hit the right talking points, focusing on the anger and angst spreading across the US. He captured an audience and his numbers rose rapidly, though he had to spend a lot of money across mediums—and I do mean *a lot* (over a billion dollars in four months!)[16]—to do so. The trend indicated his campaign approach was working... And then he stepped in front of the camera in a live debate, and it all fell apart.

There are a number of reasons that could be argued as to why Bloomberg failed so horribly in the two debates he took part in, but most of them come down to the question of authenticity. The online Bloomberg, the one touted online, was charismatic, direct, clear, and engaging, inspiring even—the Bloomberg of the debates was anything but. When he got up there on stage, he seemed uninterested, disconnected, and almost bored at times. He couldn't get his message across and his comments and quips landed flat, or didn't land at all. When he spoke, he sounded condescending or oblivious, as if he wasn't prepared or didn't care to be. There seemed to be no real compulsion for him to actually speak to, and connect with, his audience. The authenticity of his message was called into question because he was unable to speak in the voice that matched the decisive, engaged, and passionate Bloomberg online. That disconnect

---

16 Benjamin Siegel and Soo Rin Kim, "Mike Bloomberg spent more than $1 billion on four-month presidential campaign according to filing," ABC News, April 20, 2020, https://abcnews.go.com/Politics/mike-bloomberg-spent-billion-month-presidential-campaign-filing/story?id=70252435.

caused his campaign to end effectively and immediately after his second debate.

Authenticity is important in all aspects of our lives, but as leaders, it's paramount. And as Bloomberg's example has shown, authenticity can't be bought. We must have a consistent established cause, with a consistent voice and set of values that we communicate regularly, engaging others on social media through our comments, likes and posts. No matter where we are speaking to our audience, we need to make sure that our message is honest, clear, and unbreakable. If we don't convey our message with a steady tone and unwavering enthusiasm, when we attempt to connect with others on important issues, we may come across as untrustworthy, pandering, or opportunistic.

Take, for example, another US presidential candidate in 2020: Kanye West. West's brief presidential run wasn't much more than a few social media posts and announcements, and though some news outlets gave him some press, few voters seemed to care, let alone take him seriously. He had no authentic online voice to allow him to be part of this conversation. Instead, he announced his presidential bid via Twitter, jumping on the bandwagon and joining the three-ring circus that had become American politics. Had West been known for an authentic personality in US politics—a presence built with honesty and integrity over time—he could have had a chance, but he didn't. He's known as an entertainer, and that's what most people took away from his run—entertainment. Bloomberg at least *seemed* to have an authentic voice, while West never proved his authenticity in the first place.

As with much of social media, showing our authentic selves is something of a balancing act. Though we want to be an authority on a subject, we don't want to come across as one-dimensional, focusing on one specific topic alone. We must become part of the larger ecosystem surrounding a topic, developing a voice that rounds us out, allows us to deliver our opinions, and drives social conversations. This ensures that people recognize that we are holding true to the values we stand for. We need to get beyond empty marketing messages and create a real dialogue and connection with the audience. If it senses we are being inauthentic, it will quickly move on.

If we stand up and speak out about our customers' pain, for example, or the issues facing our market, we begin to engage with our audience about topics that are important to them. And we don't need a marketing conduit in the middle—we can go straight to LinkedIn, Twitter, YouTube, or any other platform. When our audience sees us talking about issues that matter, it'll ask questions like, "How do their words resonate with me? Do I believe them?" These people will want to know whether or not we're credible. If we prove that we are, they'll be willing to follow us.

As we build an audience using our own personal social media channels, we become the face and voice of the company we represent, even if we're not the "official spokespeople." Some would argue that this isn't true, that the CEO always assumes this role. Though that idea may have held water fifteen, ten, even five years ago, in this hyperconnected world today, the CEO is no longer necessarily the spokesperson. Leaders down the line may therefore end up as de facto spokespeople, especially if they can prove the authenticity of their voice. These could be VPs of a region or a vertical that handles a certain area, like global accounts. With social media, these VPs are not just talking to prospective customers, they're talking to their own employees and partners. They're actually contributing to the ecosystem where their organization fits, taking on a legitimate participatory role that allows that ecosystem to accept them as a contributing member. They are not Kanye West running for president.

Keep in mind, "real" recognizes "real." Authenticity recognizes authenticity. You can't just jump into a conversation and expect to be accepted without putting in the work, as the work is what makes you truly authentic. This work, and not necessarily what your product does or what your company provides, will inspire people. Still, you need to make sure the topics you're exploring and discussing in these conversations eventually come back to focus on your business, organization, or company in some way. But how do you ensure that what you're investing your time and effort in aligns with your company's goals and your personal goals? What lies at the heart of being authentic and what exhibits that authenticity? The answer is three simple words: your big why.

FIND YOUR BIG WHY

Author and motivational speaker, Simon Sinek, puts it clearly in his book *Start with Why*. He says, "People don't buy what you do; they buy why you do it."[17] This "big why" should act as a guiding principle in all our social media activities. It's why we do what we do. It is not simply what we're interested in and what motivates us; it's what we *contribute* to what interests and motivates us. Unfortunately, when we ask ourselves what we contribute to the social conversations around us, social media Myth #3 (Nothing Relevant to Say), often rears its ugly head, causing us to question whether or not we have anything worthwhile to contribute at all. If the answer is not staring us right in the face, then we feel like we have nothing important to say. But finding our big why isn't as hard as many of us think—we just need to uncover our true motivations and recognize others'. Afterall, leadership relies on understanding what is important to the people we're leading, as well as what's important to us.

---

17 Simon Sinek, *Start with Why: How Great Leaders Inspire Everyone to Take Action*, reprint edition (New York: Portfolio, 2011), 45.

To discover your big why, start by revisiting the self-assessment in Chapter 1, thinking this time about your true motivations and what, more than anything else, you want to contribute to the world around you. Reconsider the questions asked and the fill-in-the blank section in light of the three words "your big why." Sometimes these answers may change from the first time you filled out the assessment, and that's great—that means you're narrowing in on what's most important to you. If the answers stayed the same, that's fine too—you're already confident in how you want to present your authentic self online and what topics and themes you want to focus on.

If you're having trouble answering these questions, try seeking some external help by pulling in other voices: coworkers, friends, colleagues, people you've inspired and influenced, and people that have inspired and influenced you. Ask them what three words *they* would use to describe you. (Or if you're worried they will only tell you what you want to hear, ask one of your parents or your spouse—they'll always be honest.) If they don't use the same or similar words to those you've identified in your self-assessment, take note of their choices. Be honest with yourself: do their words describe you more accurately? Think about why certain words attach themselves to you, and what you've done throughout your career to make them stick. Keep in mind any pertinent events or experiences that you might be able to draw on later in your posts.

As discussed, we often dismiss our own experiences, ideas, and accomplishments as irrelevant. Having someone you trust to help you hone in the important things you've done throughout your career will go a long way in helping you find your big why. Retired executive vice president, Gwen McDonald, is a prime example of someone who dismissed her own experiences. Gwen has been a trailblazer and a barrier breaker for much of her career. She was the first female executive vice president at NetApp, as well as the first person of color to hold that title within the company. When Gwen first started building her digital presence using social media, she wasn't quite sure what she wanted to talk about, what conversations she wanted to engage in, how, or why. But as an executive leader and woman of color in the historically, and still predominantly white, male tech industry for over thirty years, she certainly had opinions to share. Still, she felt she needed to find some kind of higher authority to validate those opinions and other ideas—a PR team, for example, that would give her the "green light." In reality, though, her experiences made her the higher authority.

As a senior vice president at 3Com, she was well known throughout the industry. But what many of her colleagues and employees didn't know was that she'd been a major part of the Urban Challenge initiative at 3Com in the 1990s and early 2000s. This program provided grants to US cities to help them become more technologically advanced, to close technology gaps, and to substantially improve municipal services for citizens through network technology. These grants allowed cities to implement initiatives such as enriched computer programs at public schools and increased computer literacy programs in their communities.

Gwen even appeared on CSPAN in 2003, officially awarding these grants to a number of cities throughout the US that year, alongside major politicians of the day, including Mayors Willie L. Brown Jr. of San Francisco, Richard M. Daley of Chicago, Thomas M. Menino of Boston, Douglas H. Palmer of Trenton, Bill Purcell of Nashville, Anthony A. Williams of DC, and Francis G. Slay of St. Louis; Senators John Breaux of Louisiana, Hilary Rodham Clinton of New York; and US Representative Nancy Pelosi of California.[18]

---

18 C-Span, "Urban Issues: US Conference of Mayors Annual Winter Meeting," C-Span.org, originally aired January 23, 2003, https://www.c-span.org/video/?174732-1/urban-issues.

Gwen was then—as she had been in the past, and continued to be in the future—a voice in the ecosystem, and a direct participant in the tech community. Women within that community came to her to say, "Gwen, we need your voice: you have been so influential to so many of us over the years." She was a mentor; she had been part of amazing initiatives, and had a unique and important perspective stemming from her background and experience. But it wasn't until she started to ask herself, and others, these type of self-assessment questions that she was really able to articulate her big why. Her answer was: developing community support and female empowerment through tech. Like Gwen, once you've identified your big why, you'll be better situated to show your authentic self and better connect with your audience beyond the surface level. That said, even once you've discovered your big why and put it into words, you still need to decide on how to best communicate it. The right voice is essential.

CONNECT, DON'T PUSH

Social media exposes our personal activities, beliefs, and life events publicly, mixing them with our professions and careers. Though that concept may seem a little nerve-wracking, it can work to our advantage. No client, customer, or employee wants an executive to be "all business" all the time, but they also don't want a business leader to only talk about his or her personal life and beliefs. It can be a fine line to walk.

In developing an authentic voice, you must blend the personal and the professional into one holistic approach that supports your big why, creating your personal–professional brand. That means talking about issues you personally believe in, while also maintaining a strong connection to, and a focus on, professional issues and topics related to your business or organization. Therefore, it's important to consider what you're willing to share with others about yourself. Think about how you would act in "real life," in the physical world. A good guide is to imagine you're at a business networking event. What would you be comfortable sharing with the people you interact with there, some of whom you may have heard of or are familiar with but whom you have never met in person? How would you talk to them about yourself? In what way would you discuss issues facing your industry or the most recent controversies in the news?

You need to develop a sixth sense about when it's time to open up about yourself and when it's time to stick to the business at hand. It's not necessary to blatantly "always be selling" and pushing the followers to an action. In reality, by engaging with them through your personal stories and beliefs, you're building a platform that lets you sell to them, work with them, and lead them in a more meaningful, though subtle, way. No one wants to be endlessly hassled by a Needlenose Ned ("Ned the Head") Ryerson.

If you remember this character from the 1994 movie *Groundhog Day*, starring Andie MacDowell and Bill Murray—a movie that felt particularly relevant during the 2020 quarantine—you'll remember his clumsy, blunt sales technique. Though Ned hasn't seen Phil Connor (played by Murray) in years, he chases him down the street, and within less than a minute, right after sharing some colorful stories to remind Phil of who Ned is—"I did the whistling bellybutton trick at the high school talent show—bing!"—he pitches Phil on life insurance. "Do you have life insurance?" he asks. "'Cause if you do, you could always use a little more! Am I right, or am I right, or am I right? Right, right, right?"[19]

Ned is the epitome of the typical salesperson when it comes to

---

19 *Groundhog Day*, Directed by Harold Ramis, Culver City, California: Columbia Pictures, 1993, https://www.youtube.com/watch?v=XqSYC_vwhDg.

online social selling—pushing, pushing, and pushing, without ever making the very real personal connections that come from a place of authenticity. Online, these connections are possible to develop with a wider audience, one that will look to a leader it believes in— one that it finds both authoritative and personable—for advice and guidance. So just as you wouldn't whip out a sales pitch during a networking event after speaking to someone for a minute or two, you don't want to ask people to buy your products and services before truly connecting with them online (see the "Gratitude for Value" section in Chapter 1).

Many leaders, and salespeople, make this major mistake when they first start using social media tools. They believe they need to always be pitching a sale, closing a deal, or engaging in some kind of transactional discussion. But just like in real life, we are not always selling, nor should we be. We find ways to become part of conversations and activities that allow us to get to know each other, discovering common ground, ideas, and experiences we want to share. This kind of relationship—this linking and binding of common interests—allows us to engage in business and trust those we work with, those we follow, and those we lead, all with con-fidence. This is the true nature of doing business: to build up a relationship, establish trust, and then engage in a mutually beneficial exchange of goods or services. Today, this is all made possible by connecting through our personal social media accounts.

Just as people can help you find your big why, you don't have to do all of this heavy lifting on your own. Start by making a list of active leaders on social media who you admire and wish to emulate. Think about those people who share the same general, or even spe-cific ideas, opinions, and values you wish to spread. Or you could identify a number of organizations whose messages you'd like to associate with your own voice. Once identified, follow them on social media and judiciously share their content through your feeds. This reposting creates a halo effect, transferring their admirable qualities to your developing personal–professional brand.

As you begin entering social conversations, you'll quickly find that your audience is more interested in your personal voice and stories, over your professional ones. Professional stories are fine, but they're not nearly as interesting as those that are personal. What your audience wants to know is what happened to motivate you, how you responded, and what the result was. These people want to know that you've gone through something similar to what they've gone through or are going through now. They want to feel an authentic connection with you, learn about your challenges, struggles, and obstacles, and understand how you recognized opportunities to overcome them. And they want to be inspired by someone whose voice they can trust—yours.

That's not going to happen if you're just posting your company's sales and earnings, then telling people to go out and buy, buy, buy. Still, you need to always keep the professional aspect in mind. Think, how do your personal stories, opinions, and values serve your personal–professional brand? What's most important for your audience to know about you in this context? Equally, what's not important? Authenticity does not mean sharing everything; there are many aspects of your life that you'd likely prefer to keep private, and that's great. Since that's the case, it's necessary to know the difference between personal and private when developing your voice.

PERSONAL IS NOT THE SAME AS PRIVATE

There are aspects of our lives that remain separate from our work identity, and rightfully so. Sometimes this may be for the safety of ourselves and our families; or maybe we've been through harmful experiences that we're still processing and aren't willing to talk about; or maybe we simply like to compartmentalize our private lives and work lives. These reasons, and many more, are all valid. Just because we don't share the intimate details of our private lives, doesn't mean we're not being authentic.

The personal and private are easily and often considered the same online, but they are not one and the same. With a little bit of work, we can keep them separated, but to do so we must first know the difference between the two. For whatever reason, when people hear "personal" they assume "private," . Someone's favorite food is personal, whereas someone's health records are private. When making a personal, authentic connection, there's no need to share private details or information.

For example, sales enablement consultant Rana Salman, Ph.D., founder and CEO of Salman Consulting, decided she'd like to share a personal story online about running. Most of her coworkers, colleagues, employees, and customers didn't necessarily know she was an avid runner, but many people run, so this fact didn't really stand out or contribute to a direct, authentic connection with her audience. She dug a little deeper and came upon an idea: about a month earlier she had begun running without earbuds. Instead of listening to audio books, music, or podcasts, she decided to be present while she ran, listening to the sounds surrounding her instead.

For those of you who aren't runners, this may come as a surprise, but it is difficult for many runners to eliminate external distractions and/or entertainment and allow themselves to focus on the present while running. They find themselves listening to loud music, thinking and overthinking current projects, past conversations, upcoming calls, dinner plans, and everything in between. And sometimes, these thoughts cause a run, meant to relax them, to overwhelm them instead. When Rana let go of her earbuds, however, she found herself more attentive to what was around her, and she experienced a sense of clarity. Ideas began to flood in, which left her energized and excited. She was able to focus on the present and truly listen to herself. When she entered this state, she produced some of her best ideas, experienced her clearest thinking, and had her most inspirational moments.

She shared this personal story online, allowing her audience to get to know a different piece of her without revealing anything private. For example, she didn't share where she ran or when, or anything else that would impact her privacy. A few days after Rana made this post, a connection reached out to her. He was intrigued by what she had written because he also had a similar experience. This interaction wouldn't have happened if it wasn't for Rana's willingness to open up about something personal through her social media channels. By sharing a personal—not private—piece of information about herself, she allowed others to make that connection with her, and then later, share that experience as a means of continuing a business conversation.

In some cases, private details can be employed, if you're comfortable doing so, and as a means to an end. Though health records are private, if you're a cancer survivor and you discuss your experience because it fits into a larger story you want to tell, one that relates to your personal–professional brand, then that would make sense. Maybe you work for a hospital or in another health-related field. Or maybe every year you run a 5K for breast cancer awareness. Similarly, if you're a recovering alcoholic, this might not be something you want to share, unless, for example, it serves a larger purpose in connecting with your audience.

Of course, what's personal to some, may be considered private to others, so you need to decide what you feel comfortable sharing. And if you don't feel comfortable sharing any specific information, then that's okay—there are other options to connect with your audience on a personal, authentic level. Most importantly, remember that you're not just using personal content for the sake of bringing it up; you're using it to create connections so you can build your community and lead your audience. This means that you still need to differentiate between yourself as an individual and a leader. Though you should be willing to put yourself out there a bit, there's always an end goal in mind: doing business. You must therefore stay focused.

WHEN AUTHENTICITY GOES BAD

Sometimes in our effort to connect with our audience and appear uber-authentic, we make decisions that harm our brand more than help it. Hindsight is of course 20/20, but if we can get in front of our mistakes, we can hopefully avoid them in the first place. When it comes to signaling our authenticity, we need to stay focused, meaning that even though we want to share ourselves with our audience, we also want to make sure we do so in an appropriate way, eventually connecting back to our business, company, or organization. Otherwise, authenticity can go bad.

For example, unless you sell hunting apparel, there's no reason the headshot in your LinkedIn profile should be of you decked out in camo from head to toe and holding a rifle. Your customers, clients, colleagues, and employees are going to look you up, and this is not the first impression you'll want to share. Such a photo would feel out of place and almost disorienting. Think about what you would be saying with this image: How does it relate to your business? How does it reflect your leadership experience and your ability to lead others? Most likely, it doesn't do a very good job.

The optics would also be that you have an agenda. By posting this photo without any context, you're not sharing a full story or opinion, but it does seem like you're pushing an idea onto your audience. Such a photo doesn't serve a larger, related purpose, and it may resonate negatively with those people you're most trying to influence. You could argue, "Well that's who I am," and that's fine—but not in this context. And if you don't care about the optics, then you're probably leading the wrong organization to begin with. You don't need to be disingenuous, and you don't need to hide who you are, but you must lead with your authentic self in a way that connects with your values and the values of your organization. Your personal beliefs or stories should support your professional presence, not the other way around. (Chapter 4 details the type of headshot photo you *should* use in your LinkedIn profile.)

There is, however, one caveat to this advice: there may be a time when you need to come to terms with the fact that your personal beliefs *do* exclude you from being authentic within your organization and career. If that's the case, you need to reevaluate your online presence and persona. Let's create an imaginary scenario. Imagine that you're Noel White, the CEO of Tyson Foods, and you've become a PETA proponent, feeling the need to comment on the harmful effects of meat production on animals and the environment—well, you get the picture. In that situation, Noel White would not be able to speak authentically to his audience, or he'd have to face any repercussions and fallouts if he were to, for example, change his headshot on LinkedIn to the words "Meat is Murder."

Another way that authenticity can go bad is through the use of humor. Even in person, humor is tricky, and it can easily go awry—it's ten times more likely to do so online. Humor is usually contextual. If it's something you're known for, you might be able to get away with it, but most leaders should not consider it as a regular approach. You're a business leader, not a comedian. Humor often relies on sarcasm, and sarcasm does not work on social media, just as it doesn't work in a text or an email. If you can't actually hear the tone of the person making "the joke" you may have no idea it's a joke at all. No matter how hard we try, some statements just don't translate well in the digital world. So, stay away from humor. Speak honestly, with authenticity, and don't try to hide behind a joke. There's a whole slew of people who do not understand this principle, so once you do, you'll already be a step ahead of them.

CONCLUSION

Most all of us can tell when someone is being inauthentic, when they're not speaking with their true voice. What do we truly know about Ned Ryerson in *Groundhog Day*? Nothing really. He sells insurance, can make his belly button whistle, had a bad case of the shingles his senior year of high school, and he *really* wants to make a sale. Then again, the same can be said for Phil Connors throughout the first half of the movie—he's anything but authentic. He's shallow, only a front. It's when he goes through a journey of self-discovery that he can actually share who he truly is. After he becomes comfortable with himself, he becomes a true leader in the town. People look to him for help and advice, and he knows what people want and how to connect with them, whether that's by giving a young newly married couple tickets to WrestleMania or playing piano to an adoring audience. In the process, he becomes a real part of the community.

That's what an authentic voice gives us the opportunity to do—connect with others and build a community around what's important to us and to the organization. We must understand what motivates us and how that motivation can affect our audience. In discovering our big why, we provide ourselves with a way to frame the topics we want to discuss, the causes we want to support and be known for, and an honest voice, one that can't simply be bought (even with a billion dollars). Still, speaking with authenticity and exposing our authentic selves is something of a balancing act. We want to be an authority on a subject, but we don't want to seem one-dimensional. We want to talk about issues that are personal and dear to us, but also relate them to what we do professionally. And we never want to give away private details.

In today's social media world, it is our credibility and authenticity that generates the most trust from our audience, and we must protect it. If people think we're pushing an agenda or are only out to make a quick buck, they will never give us the support we need to conduct our business or create lasting change. We must prove our authenticity, wisely choosing the brands and causes we wish to associate with. We must work tirelessly to be seen as genuine leaders who stand for what we believe in. Dishonesty and insincerity can be sniffed out quickly by online communities and can have devastating effects, so authenticity is absolutely central to our social media communication and digital presence.

CHAPTER 3

SET YOURSELF APART AND STAND OUT FROM THE CROWD

ON JUNE 2, 2020, in lieu of the typical light-hearted images and marketing ads posted on Instagram every day, over 28 million users posted a simple black box—no photos and no text, aside from hashtags such as "#BlackLivesMatter" and "#BlackoutTuesday."[20] Anyone following the news of the previous week would have rightly assumed that this mass online act came as a statement in response to the killing of an unarmed Black man, named George Floyd, by four police officers. Protests against police brutality and systemic racism quickly followed Floyd's death—first locally, then nationally, then internationally—causing conversations about the past, current, and future treatment of Black Americans, and the inequalities and injustices they have consistently faced in the US, to take center stage.

20 Paul Monckton, "This Is Why Millions of People Are Posting Black Squares On Instagram," *Forbes*, June 22, 2020, https://www.forbes.com/sites/paulmonckton/2020/06/02/blackout-tuesday-instagram-black-squares-blackouttuesday-theshowmustbepaused.

When these boxes started popping up in a show of solidarity across social media, many companies joined in.

The boxes were effective, providing an accessible and somewhat casual way for millions of individuals and organizations to show their support for the Black Lives Matter movement and take the opportunity to publicly foster dialogues on race in America. One company, however, took a different, more aggressive approach. If you were to have looked at the Ben & Jerry's Instagram page that day, you would have seen a black box as well, but with the words "We Must Dismantle White Supremacy" emblazoned across it in big, bold lettering, the font in "White Supremacy" crumbling away. The company did not mince words; they were not subtle in the slightest. The power of their statement was unique and impossible to misinterpret, especially as they supplemented the post with the following caption: "The murder of George Floyd was the result of inhumane police brutality that is perpetuated by a culture of white supremacy." They then provided a link for a full statement on Floyd's death and four policy proposals they believed had to be undertaken immediately in response.[21]

Though some may have been surprised by the corporation's swift and unequivocal response, Ben & Jerry's was far from new to weighing in on the social and political issues of the day. Four years earlier, in 2016, they also voiced their support for the Black Lives Matter movement, which was then still burgeoning.[22] However, that is just one example in a long line of purposeful, powerful statements and actions the company has taken in support of its values, dating back to its founding in 1978 by Ben Cohen and Jerry Greenfield.

---

21 Ben & Jerry's, "We Must Dismantle White Supremacy: Silence Is Not An Option," benjerry.com, June 2, 2020, https://www.benjerry.com/about-us/media-center/dismantle-white-supremacy.

22 Ben & Jerry's, "Black Lives Matter: Why Black lives matter," benjerry.com, October 6, 2016, https://www.benjerry.com/whats-new/2016/why-black-lives-matter.

Their socially and environmentally conscious beliefs have always been a bedrock of the company, and even after selling it to Unilever in 2000, this same spirit has remained intact. For example, Ben & Jerry's is a certified B-Corporation, one of only around 3,500 businesses that are "legally required to consider the impact of their decisions on their workers, customers, suppliers, community, and the environment."[23] And when it comes to social, political, or environmental issues, their leadership openly and directly talks about them.

Ben & Jerry's current CEO Matthew McCarthy stated that the death of George Floyd was "piercing that false veil between our human lives and our business lives."[24] Not only was his authenticity on display, melding the personal and professional, but he spoke to both the overall business environment and his community.[25] Instead of relying on fly-by-night bandwagon corporate messaging, McCarthy followed the Ben & Jerry's playbook established by Cohen and Greenfield years earlier, engaging the audience with an authentic voice. The community surrounding Ben & Jerry's has therefore come to trust what the company's leaders say, believing in the honesty of their message.

But their ability to connect with their audience and amplify an authentic voice comes from a willingness to set themselves apart and stand out from the crowd. If you take a look at the Ben & Jerry's Instagram account, you'll still see posts on new flavors and classic ones, but you'll also find posts on social issues related to dismantling white supremacy. These include posts about mass incarceration, the

---

23 Certified B Corporation, "A Global Community of Leaders," bcorporation.net, accessed September 22, 2020.
24 Melissa Repko, "Ben & Jerry's CEO: 'Business must be held accountable' in setting specific goals to fight racism."
25 Melissa Repko, "Ben & Jerry's CEO: 'Business must be held accountable' in setting specific goals to fight racism."

history of Black oppression, front end criminal justice reform, systemic racism, and reparations. Their values are not a flash in the pan, and they speak them boldly, without reserve or fear of consequences. How many corporations or leaders could we say the same about today?

Getting over our fears and misunderstandings about social media and deciding on the content we want to be known for and share—as is outlined in Chapters 1 and 2—are the first steps to becoming true digital-first leaders. But we can't stop there. We can only develop a community and tribe, an audience willing to follow us, if we make sure we set ourselves apart from the other leaders out there. We don't all need to run companies like Ben & Jerry's, or make consistent bold statements on social issues, but we can find ways to ensure our voices are heard and that we remain part of the many conversations constantly taking place. To do so, we must take an approach of predictability, persistence, and presence in our use of social media, providing us with the ability to respond to crises and seize opportunities in real time and build our brand over the long term. Luckily, even by just using these tools, we've already begun setting ourselves apart from other leaders.

PARTICIPATION INEQUALITY

Leaders like Matthew McCarthy have an often-overlooked advantage with their digital presence, though it is by no means particular to a well-established brand like Ben & Jerry's, that is, participation inequality. Participation inequality refers to the idea that whenever we're in groups, big or small, there is a tendency for a subset of that group to more actively engage than the rest of us in the conversations and activities taking place. When we're in groups, the natural human behavior is for most to stay quiet at first, letting only a few people to participate in what's happening. There's usually a single individual among us who, by being the first to speak up, ends up driving the whole discussion. Participation inequality can be found in focus groups, in classrooms, on sports teams, and at work—this hierarchy develops naturally when people interact with each other.

Participation inequality is especially present online, though we may not recognize it. Most of us think that everyone is already using social media, even if we aren't or if we're novices at best. But while it appears that there is a large group of people generating original content online, only a small percentage of any group actually does so—the vast majority of members are passive participants, meaning they're not engaging with others on anything more than a surface level.

The participation inequality issue is referred to as the 90-9-1 rule (or the 1 percent rule), where 90 percent of participants passively consume content without contributing (also known as lurkers); 9 percent participate occasionally, responding to or commenting on that content; and only 1 percent create original content, putting forth new ideas and suggestions, posting original material, commenting regularly, and driving conversations.[26] Let's break that down. Say you have 1,000 connections via LinkedIn. Of those connections, 900 will be lurkers, 90 will be somewhat active, and 10 will actually be engaged participants. You should be one of those ten.

Leaders, particularly at the C-Suite level, are part of a small group of individuals, and within this group, only a tiny fraction are creating original online content. Though LinkedIn has 600 million accounts (sounds like a lot, right?), each one of us on the platform is probably only connected to a few thousand. Even if you're connected to 10,000 people, you'd still only be one of a hundred who are actively creating and posting content, and that's where you have your

---

26 Jakob Nielsen, "The 90-9-1 Rule for Participation Inequality in Social Media and Online Communities," Nielsen Norman Group, October 8, 2006, https://www.nngroup.com/articles/participation-inequality/.

edge over the other 9,900 luddite leaders who still think LinkedIn is only for job hunting.

Therefore, when we create content, engage with others, and participate in conversations, we're not actually competing with all of the noise out there in the overcrowded digital environment. We're really only competing with a small percentage of other leaders, since so many have yet to develop their social media fluency and digital presence. The audience who coalesces around us will also naturally fall along the lines of participation inequality, meaning even if there are multiple leaders in our community or tribe, when we take the initiative to step out and be vocal, we stand out simply because there are a few other people doing the same.

Keep in mind the organization we work for and the products and services we offer are almost always somewhat niche—in Ben & Jerry's case, there are only so many ice cream manufacturers; they're not competing for the same audience as Samsung and LG. This further decreases the size of the audience and community, which means we're competing with even less leaders. Since we're all members of a specific industry, however, we may have a misperception that our peers, colleagues, and competitors are already creating and dispersing the content that we might want to create. We think, "everybody else is already doing it," but that's mostly because we're connected to those people who are part of similar industries, networking circles, and business spheres.

If, for example, you're a social media coach with a focus on LinkedIn—and I fully admit I'm speaking from personal experience here—when you take the temperature of the digital atmosphere, you're going to struggle with the assumption that *everybody* out there is a LinkedIn coach and professional. But you have to remind yourself, "Well, yeah, duh, everyone looks like they're in this space because I'm in a network of a bunch of LinkedIn coaches—of course we're covering similar content." In the meantime, your customers are looking for the solutions that you and your colleagues provide, and on the whole, there really aren't *that* many of you in this area when all is said and done. There are more than enough ways to distinguish the content you produce and the audience you connect with, but there's no way for you to do this unless you first participate.

We can easily see the exceptions among executive figures who create significant levels of content on a regular basis. These are leaders like Richard Branson, Bill Gates, Warren Buffett, and John Legere. As the former CEO of T-Mobile, Legere spent six to seven hours a day using social media while he was the head of the telecommunications giant.[27] He also refused to farm out his social interaction to the PR department or anyone else, saying "You know one of the things you can't do in social is, it has to be you, if it ever becomes—and they can tell—if it's somebody being you, they vote you off the island."[28] Today, Legere continues to personally engage his 6.2 million followers on Twitter. Most executives won't become Legere, but if they regularly produce online content, their behavior is already an outlier compared to that of the majority of other executives. Their status as C-Suite executives also gives them a platform that other leaders do not have, and since so few of Branson's, Gates's, Buffett's, and Legere's peers take advantage of this platform, simply being active on social media solidly places these four (and others like them) as part of that unique 1 percent.

As discussed in Chapter 1, social media is not meant to only be consumed. It's meant to create engagement, involvement, and

---

27 Lucy Handley, "This top CEO is good friends with Snoop Dogg and spends most of his working day on Twitter," CNBC.com, November 3, 2017, https://www.cnbc.com/2017/11/03/t-mobile-ceo-john-legere-spends-most-of-his-working-day-on-twitter.html.

28 Lucy Handley, "This top CEO is good friends with Snoop Dogg and spends most of his working day on Twitter"

activity, all of which help you lead. But if you sit out on the sidelines, how will you practice your leadership? A LinkedIn profile or a Twitter handle are only as good as you make them. Participation inequality is your secret weapon to success on social media—if you don't actively participate, then your social media platforms become a stagnant waste of digital space. Just by participating you have a leg up, but once you do, it's time to take your engagement to the next level, so you can stand out among the 1 percent of participants. To do that, you must follow participation with three more "P"s.

THE THREE PS OF STANDING OUT FROM THE CROWD

Predictability, persistence, and presence are the three Ps that help us stand out from the crowd to build our audience and lead our community. The three Ps ensure that our voices are not just active, but actively heard. When people respond, a conversation begins, creating the engagement we're after. This engagement prepares us to respond to crises and seize opportunities when they arise, but these responses will only be effective if we have already reached our audience. The middle of a crisis is not the time to begin building our online presence. If the first Instagram post Ben & Jerry's ever made was about white supremacy, they would have likely had to fight an uphill battle for credibility. By being regular participants in social conversations, however, they were able to make a bold statement that their audience believed was truly theirs. And in so doing, they only established their unique positioning further. The three Ps allow all of us to legitimately participate in social conversations that build up a reputation we can leverage to our advantage. The problem is, they are rarely followed, even by leaders creating online content. Let's take a deeper look at that they mean, beginning with "predictability."

PREDICTABILITY

Predictability means we produce and post content that appears on such a regular basis, that our audience begins to anticipate it, look for it, and expect it. Think of throwback Thursdays (TBT) or flashback Fridays (FBF); these have become established, expected posts for many users' followers. We can develop a cadence of the material we share, whether it's once a day, once a week, or once a month. The more frequent our posts, the easier it is to grow our audience. A predictable schedule of content creates an expectation in our audience that it will continue to see material from us on a regular basis. Like with TBT or FBF, our followers begin to internalize our content as part of their own schedules and routines. As with selling a product or service, we have to create expectations that will lead to anticipation.

When it comes to LinkedIn, the predictability of our content is incredibly important because the app's algorithm rewards it. The LinkedIn algorithm ensures that whenever we gain new contacts, any content we post appears to these connections in the first week after we've connected with them. In that sense, LinkedIn gives a higher priority to the people we "just met." If those new connections engage with the content we post on LinkedIn—whether it's a podcast, article, blog, or regular column—LinkedIn will make sure it's initially visible to them. If this engagement continues, over time the audience will come to expect it. Once the algorithm recognizes that our content is resonating with our followers, it begins to curate our content to them, causing the material to be more predictable. This algorithm essentially creates a cycle: as our contacts receive new content from us, they begin to expect it, and as long as we produce it, the algorithm continues to share it.

This type of predictability also creates an online halo effect of sorts, in which our regular participation over time creates the impression that we're still producing and sharing content, even when we're not. This approach comes, in part, from the ad world. Advertising agencies sometimes run an ad in a weekly magazine every week for about six weeks. Running this ad on an aggressive schedule early in a campaign creates an accelerated cadence and a rapid familiarization with the audience. Then the agency starts running the ad every other week, then maybe just once a month.

The agency's audience is now so used to seeing this ad every week, it begins to blend into the background of its consciousness. Members of the audience, which have grown, don't notice the deceleration of the ad's appearance, but instead, mentally fill in the gaps of when the ad would have normally appeared. They might make an unconscious assumption that they simply missed the previous ad, or convince themselves that they saw it, when in reality they didn't. These ads become such an expected part of their routine, so much that they seem to exist even when they don't.

This same concept can be applied to your social media activities. If your audience members become used to seeing your content in their feeds on a regular basis, the halo effect causes them to believe you are there, sharing content all the time, even when you're not. Initially, you will have to post often, but in time, you will be able to reduce that cadence to a more manageable frequency, which also won't require as much effort. Having this touch point of consistent, widespread material allows you to set up an expectation in the minds of your followers. They won't just look for your content but will be psychologically drawn to it, as it has become a regularly occurring part of their day, week, or month. Still, this predictability cannot be developed over night; it also requires time to become effective, which is why the second P, persistence, is so important. While predictability looks to the future, persistence speaks more to the past.

PERSISTENCE

Persistence requires a demonstrated willingness to put out content that matters. We must show we're in this social media game for the long haul, proving to our followers that we have been there for them in the past, are here for them now, and will be there for them in the future. In return, they will make an emotional investment in following us, listening to us, and engaging with us. Our persistence communicates that we are invested in our followers as much as we are expecting them to be invested in us.

Persistence also implies longevity. No one will listen to what we have to say if we only pop in occasionally to throw our hat into the ring on a major debate, or to simply comment on a topic, then go radio silent again. We must be active, as this builds our credibility when we join a social conversation and want our voice heard. If a topic we regularly talk about is in the spotlight and we chime in to give our opinion, the audience knows our thoughts and words are not just a gimmick. Similar to tribe building (discussed in Chapter 2), we must prove we've been doing this for a long time, that we are part of the ecosystem. This persistence is what separates legitimate thought leaders from the opportunistic ones. But persistence isn't easy.

The internet is littered with the social media detritus of well-intentioned efforts. It's become a graveyard of once good ideas, old blog posts, defunct YouTube channels, and abandoned podcasts, clogging up digital channels and online searches. Nothing is more frustrating than to emotionally invest in a medium of content only to have it prematurely end. Sometimes our efforts just don't pan out like we'd hoped, and as leaders who are used to success, the experience can be frustrating. But if we give up and revert to our old ways, we'll never get to the point where our audience will take us seriously. And as discussed, the less we prove that we're able to use today's communication and leadership tools, the more our audience will begin to wonder if we're true leaders at all. If we persist, however, and are able to showcase this persistence, our audience is much more likely to follow us.

Though persistence is a mindset we must develop, we can help ourselves get there by setting up a routine for our social media usage, which also contributes to the first P, predictability. Creating a schedule to practice regularly and frequently is crucial here, as social media influence and effectiveness take time. Like any other habit or exercise, we have to continue to work on the act, think about it, and then actually do it, before we start to get the feel for it. In the case of developing a social media routine, the purpose is to connect with and lead our audience. If our engagement with our audience and efforts to maintain its attention isn't regular, we will ultimately fail.

THE ROUTINE OF PERSISTENCE

So much of social media is perceived as random 2 a.m. tweets or half-thought-out sentiments dashed off and posted without a moment of reflection (or proofreading). There are many leaders who understand the point of social media, but who still approach it this way. Unfortunately, if you're not using these tools systematically and strategically, then it's almost like you're not using them at all. Taking an approach to your social media practices without rhyme or reason means you'll never get the type of awesome response that is otherwise possible.

"What about the content itself?" some might argue. "My content is the best! Who cares when I post it?" Sure, content is king, but only if people are actually engaging with it. Think about the kindling needed to build a fire. If you've ever attempted to light a match to a pile of small sticks, you know that the distance between the sticks is important. If the kindling is too close, it doesn't allow in enough air to fuel the fire, which suffocates the match. And if the kindling is too far apart, the fire isn't able to feed off of itself and it will quickly go out. Your social media activity can be seen in the same way—post too much and you smother your audience with content, or too sparsely and you're not able to build up a cycle at all. You must therefore establish guidelines that allow you to regularly create and share content on whichever social media platform you have chosen.

Start by determining the amount of time you can commit to using social media. With more time comes more effectiveness, but that doesn't mean you have to put in the same tremendous number of hours as John Legere to make an impact on your audience (recall the seven-minute rule from Chapter 1). You have several options: you can post or share content every day, every week, every two weeks, or once a month. More engagement means faster growth, especially earlier on, and it will lead to more influence over the conversations you are participating in. Keep in mind, there is also a lead up to posting the content. You first need to create it or curate it. As discussed in Chapter 1, before you're generating original content, you'll likely start using social media tools by reposting or commenting on content that is already out there.

With that in mind, consider keeping a running list of content you may want to share with your audience. There are curation tools, like Pocket (www.getpocket.com), that can help, allowing you to collect content that you read online by tagging it and categorizing it. This tool, and other similar ones, also provides recommendations based on what other people are collecting. As such, if you come across an interesting article online that relates to your specific company or industry, or one that is more widely connected with your big why, you can tag the piece with Pocket. The app will then place it in a collection point accessible from your computer or mobile device.

Then, at a designated time (say every Sunday evening before your workweek), you can go through the material to decide what exactly to share, pulling out the content you feel will most resonate with your audience. Once you have the content curated and identified, you can then use time-shifting tools that allow you to schedule your posts for the same time every day, week, or month. These time-shifting tools, like Buffer and Hootsuite, let you pre schedule the release of your post. So, after you've written out your comments about an article, for instance, your words, along with the media or link that goes with them, will all be posted at the predetermined time. These tools are also useful in scheduling any original content you'd like to post on a prescheduled, regular basis.

If you're at the point where you're using multiple social media tools (discussed in Chapter 4), choose a day and time when you want your content to go live on these different platforms. Traditionally, research shows that the most effective time for posting content is 1 p.m. to 3 p.m. on a Wednesday, followed by 6 a.m. to 8 a.m. on a Tuesday, 8 a.m. to 10 a.m. on a Wednesday, and 11 a.m. to 1 p.m. on a Thursday.[29] You will notice that Monday, Friday, and the weekend are missing from this list. A key to being successful with sharing your content is to post when people will most likely engage with it. Before the changes brought about by Covid-19, Mondays and Fridays were usually distracting days, though for opposite reasons: on Mondays, everyone tried to catch up on work, and on Fridays, everyone just looked forward to escaping work.

Since the Covid-19 pandemic, however, these rules have not held. For example, previously, the conventional wisdom was to not post material during commuting hours, since most people were

---

29 Elizabeth Arens, "The best times to post on social media in 2020," sproutsocial.com, August 3, 2020, https://sproutsocial.com/insights/best-times-to-post-on-social-media/.

listening to podcasts, the news, or music, while driving or taking public transportation. The idea was therefore to post before or after commuting hours or at lunch, when people were taking a break or not rushing to get to or from work, their attention elsewhere. Now that so many people are working from home, most of these rules have gone out the window. There are no more commute times. Many of us are in front of computers or smartphones no matter what time of day, and even on the weekends—maybe even *more so* on the weekends, as our options of what to do with our free time have drastically dwindled. This change means that there are no longer any hard and fast rules on when to post material, so you need to decide what's best for you in this new reality. What matters most is that you're sharing content on a regular basis.

Scheduling your social media activities in advance helps contribute to a cadence of material that builds predictability and makes sure your voice is heard. Finding the flow to put the content out there can be challenging, but remind yourself that your team, employees, and customers are looking for you to share your thoughts. Once you put together a plan of attack, you can almost automate the ability to share your experiences, expertise, and insights with your growing tribe. Yes, there's still the back-end work of identifying and creating content, but the schedule is what will get your content in front of your audience like clockwork. This will also free up some time, and mental space, for you to focus on the third P: presence.

PRESENCE

Presence represents the idea that our content should be showing up in multiple places, or what are referred to as "social proof points." Social proof points reinforce that as leaders, we're not engaging with our audience in a narrow window or in an environment we've somehow controlled. They prove that our content is widely available online through numerous channels, reaching all the members of our current and potential audience. When our followers see us commenting on another users' Twitter post, joining a social conversation on LinkedIn, responding to a critique or criticism on a YouTube video, or sharing our thoughts through a blog that is reposted and boosted by our readers, they begin to recognize that we have something worthy to contribute.

If we profess to be experts or thought leaders, and our followers are truly interested in who we are, what we have to say, and how we might be able to connect or collaborate, then they'll want to know as much about us as possible. They'll go online to see our social proof points and gauge our digital presence. When they do that, they need to find us *everywhere*—this is true presence. In the early Internet era, before social media became so ubiquitous, we made sure our audience could find us, our products, and our services, using search engine optimization (SEO). Through SEO, we created content in such a way that search engines would index it, then deliver it in search results for those looking for it. The idea was that we would tailor our content to be optimized for maximum indexing and exposure.

Today, SEO is not as important as it once was. Our content must now show up wherever our followers are looking, instead of them having to look for it. The first reason is that some users just prefer one platform over another. It's not uncommon to have followers who only use one, and even if they're on others, they may not check them regularly. This decision could come down to personal preference, time constraints, applicability to their industry or job, or a whole number of other reasons. Whatever it is, this means you need to be present across different platforms.

The second reason comes down to basic online competition. Platforms like Facebook don't want their users to resort to Google in search for specific content as this would take them off the platform and reduce ad revenue. They don't want to lose their users as customers for even that fraction of a second. Instead, platforms like Facebook strive to deliver to users the content they believe users will find most interesting, based on their own algorithms and the other content shared by their users. When our followers use Facebook, they may get stuck in a blackhole of Facebook content, from which they need to actively remove themselves. If our content is not present in that blackhole, they may never see it.

This isn't only true for Facebook—the same is true for Twitter, Instagram, YouTube, and most social media platforms. Rather than create their own content, or drive us to another location, they rely on the concept that their users will generate the content and deliver it themselves, using the crowd to build demand and provide the metrics for which relevant content should be shared. For our content to be considered worth following, it must therefore show up in the places where our followers are spending their time. Our content should find them, meeting them where they already are. Social media is, of course, where the people are, which is one of the reasons leaders need to be active online, growing their digital presence in the first place. It calls to mind words of wisdom from famed bank robber, Willie Sutton, who reportedly replied to an interviewer's question about why he robbed banks by saying, "because that's where the money is." The same can be said for social media today, but if we're only present on one platform, we massively limit our audience.

Every time our content is liked, shared, or commented on, it is spread far beyond our personal network. This is the type of presence we should be striving for; we want our content to be viewed multiple times by the same followers in more than one place. Once they see it enough times, and readily share it with their friends and contacts, it will eventually bubble up to cross a threshold of relevance. At this point, we begin to truly connect with a wider audience. This (omni) presence plays back into predictability and persistence—if our content is expected, consistent, and available anywhere our audience may already be, we guarantee ourselves the opportunity to communicate, connect, and lead. The three Ps take foresight and discipline, but they will allow you to do more than you ever expected as a digital-first leader. And since they are difficult to get down pat, not many leaders follow through on them. Therefore, just by following through, you set yourself apart and create a space—multiple spaces in fact—to share your voice, opinions, and ideas.

CONCLUSION

If we, as leaders. persistently speak out about the issues and values we hold dear, we establish our right to talk about an even wider range of topics when they arise. It could be the entrenched pay gap between men and women, gun violence, or healthcare—it doesn't matter. If we're willing to make a stand in a unique or otherwise unexpected way, we highlight what sets us apart from other digital-first leaders and gives us a seat at the social conversation table. It's no wonder companies like Ben & Jerry's can speak out with an authentic voice on nearly any topic they feel the need to talk about—they have a long, steady history of doing just that. They know their employees and customers are behind them, so they're willing to take risks. Then again, Ben & Jerry's is a true outlier, there are very few companies "like" it, and this is what gives its leaders the flexibility to support their values with the bold attitude their audience has come to trust.

We can only follow their example if we use social media tools, create original content, and get it out to an expectant audience. If we place ourselves in the 1 percent of content creators, and not the passive consumers, we also place ourselves at the forefront of any social conversation we'd like to be a part of, whether it relates directly or indirectly to our business or industry. Once we're participating, we must use the three Ps—predictability, persistence, and presence—to create a steady social media routine to further develop our use of these tools, which in turn, develops our digital-first leadership capabilities. When done correctly, we are then positioned to respond to opportunities and crises as they occur, increasing our engagement with our audience and allowing us to lead with confidence and credibility when it counts the most.

CHAPTER 4

LEARN THE TOOLS

IF YOU'LL EXCUSE my self-indulgence for a moment, I have a personal story—though not a private one (see Chapter 2 on the difference)—I'd like to share. Though I'm originally from Olympia, Washington, I've traveled the world and lived in many places, including San Diego, California. I grew up with a number of siblings; one happens to be named John. And, as mentioned in the Introduction, up until I transitioned into my current career, I'd worked in marketing and the tech industry for years. What does any of this have to do with becoming a digital-first leader? Well, if you Google "Richard Bliss San Diego," the first result will likely grab your attention.

You'll find a Wikipedia entry for Richard Bliss, from Olympia, Washington, who, while living in San Diego and working in the tech industry in the 1990s, was arrested in November 1997 in Russia on charges of espionage. His brother John is listed as speaking with the press and claiming that Richard is not, in fact, a spy. The President of the United States and the US Secretary of State had to intervene in the situation. After eleven days of being held by Russian authorities, without toilet facilities or the ability to speak to anyone, only given bread to eat and water to drink, Richard was released from prison with instructions to never return to Russia.

What makes this story absolutely amazing is that it is all true… but this Richard Bliss is not me. When Richard Bliss was arrested in Russia, my mother called me, wondering where I was. I was living in Dayton, Ohio, actively running a company, but she wanted to know if I was the Richard in Russia. Let me tell you something: if your mother ever calls you because she's concerned you may have been arrested as a spy, and she's worried you're rotting away in a Russian prison cell, while you're actually hanging out at your home in the American Midwest, you know your online narrative has gone far beyond your ability to control it. But she wasn't the only one; the press even began to call, wanting to know if I was *the* Richard Bliss.

Though this event took place over twenty years ago, it has continued to influence my life to this very day. For example, in the tech industry, when you apply for a job at a multibillion, multinational corporation, they do a security background check to make sure there is nothing of concern in your past. From 1997 on, whenever I applied to a tech job, I had to warn every potential employer that I was going to fail the background check. Sure enough, every time I failed, they had to delay my hiring and extend the investigation beyond the normal measures. Yes, 1997 was before social media—and actually before the Internet had really taken off to become what it is today—but twenty-plus years later, my online reputation and digital presence continues to be impacted by an event that had nothing to do with me. It's not uncommon for me to mention this story to prospective clients, not just because it showcases the importance of controlling our online narratives and digital presence, but also because I know when they Google me they'll find this Wiki entry and wonder if they're dealing with a former CIA spook.

Our online reputation is rapidly becoming more prominent; who we are, how we are perceived, and how we lead, all come down to our digital presence. To maintain this presence, we need to get ourselves some "virtual real estate." We know what real estate is all about, right? Location, location, location. We must stake out our corner of the digital world and identify it as ours. If we don't, our desired narrative about who we are, as individuals and leaders, may be lost in the confusion of misinformation. And when we lose control of our own narrative, we lose control of our ability to lead. To ensure this doesn't happen, we need to get down to the nuts and bolts of actually setting up and using these social media tools. From there, we can begin to develop a cadence of use and, over time, master it.

Of course, we don't need to perfect our knowledge of each tool right away, but we do need to know the basics, specifically of the big four: LinkedIn, Twitter, Instagram, and Facebook. In addition to the "big four," remember that blog posts; podcasts; bylined online articles; YouTube and TikTok videos; and even crowdfunding platforms, like GoFundMe, are all forms of social media. Though each platform has its own quirks and specific purposes, when strategically used together, they help develop a robust online presence. We must therefore create a balance between them. Still, LinkedIn is where people actually do business, so it's the main social media tool that business leaders use. With that in mind, let's start there.

LINKEDIN

Many leaders mistakenly believe that they don't really *use* LinkedIn—they create a profile and then move on, setting and then forgetting it. But once they set up that profile, they *do* use LinkedIn on a regular basis—every single day. We all do. We may just not know it. As part of our digital presence, our LinkedIn profiles are on display whenever someone sits down at their computer or unlocks their smartphone and Googles our names. Our customers (current and potential), fellow colleagues, and employees all look at them. This immediate accessibility must make us consider what we want them to see, at any given moment of any given day.

LinkedIn is the bedrock of virtual real estate when it comes to doing business; it presents an opportunity to engage around specific topics, thoughts, or ideas that are common in the companies, organizations, and industries we lead. Not all of us have Facebook, not all of us have Instagram, and not all of us have Twitter, but all of us have LinkedIn—or at least we should. Why? Because we're in business. Whether we have a job or looking for a job, we must always have a digital presence that speaks of who we are as leaders. As discussed in the Introduction, LinkedIn is the center of our digital identity, so we can't skimp on the details when it comes to creating our profile and correctly using the platform. Getting the key components just right is essential.

HEADSHOT

The headshot is the first element of your profile that your followers will pay attention to. That's right, they'll scrutinize your face, trying to decide if they believe they can trust you to be the professional leader you purport to be. Whether or not this knee-jerk assessment of your mug is fair, it's going to happen. Since that's the case, you have to use an image that conveys trust, concern with appearances, and a level of formality. Sure, if you're a professional clown, formality may be less of a concern, but you better appear in costume, friendly, fun-loving, and entertaining—nobody's going to hire you if you look like Pennywise from Stephen King's *It*. Point being, the photo should be appropriate for your profile and brand.

The headshot doesn't necessarily need to be taken by a professional, but it should look good. Use natural lighting; avoid grainy, blurry, or out-of-focus photos; and make sure the headshot is high-res. Also, be honest with yourself when it's time to update your photo. You'll be on LinkedIn for many years to come, so the headshot should be relevant to your age and representative of your current appearance. Don't use a photo that's more than five years old.

Furthermore, don't obscure your face with sunglasses, a baseball cap, a helmet, or any other type of protective gear. Even if you're a big skier, your face shouldn't be hidden under a scarf, knit hat, and goggles. If your followers can't see what you look like, they aren't going to trust you. Similarly, don't use a photo that has obviously been cropped from your wedding or another event. Though you may look great in that particular picture, cropped images come across as sloppy and unprofessional. And speaking of unprofessional, save the relaxed shot of yourself taken at the local bar on a Sunday afternoon for your private scrapbook. Your followers want to feel confident in your abilities as a leader, and no matter how much they might like to have a drink every now and again, if you give them the impression that most of your time leading is spent bellying up to the bar, their confidence in you will likely diminish quickly.

Finally, make sure the photo is of you and you alone. Don't include an image with your pets, family, significant other, or kids. Some leaders might push back on this idea, arguing that they're "family men and women," or that their significant others are the most important people in the world to them, or that they absolutely love their pets. Well, think of it this way: If you were to meet a new employee, a potential client, or another senior leader for the first time, would you start pulling out photos of your family, or your pets, before you've even introduced yourself? It's important to consider what we want to achieve with the headshot we're sharing, which is something many of us often forget. It's not "all about us"—it's about connecting with the audience. Today, this is how we first and foremost make our first impression, so we need to remain focused. Remember, LinkedIn is all business, so a headshot fitting to our business and career is a must.

BANNER IMAGE

The banner image appears in the large backdrop at the top of your LinkedIn profile. This image provides an opportunity to visually brand yourself in a way that creates a connection between you and your audience. The banner sets the tone of your profile, indicating how you want to be identified and perceived, and therefore, it should be both relevant and eye-catching. For example, if you live in an interesting geographic or otherwise immediately recognizable region of the world, you can draw upon its iconic imagery, like the Golden Gate Bridge in San Francisco, the skyline of New York City, or the Himalayas in Nepal. Using a photo that connects with your customers and prospects in the targeted geographical region—say the sun rising over the beaches of Cape Cod if your clients are in southeastern Massachusetts—works well too.

You could also use imagery related to the industry you're in: if you're a writer, use a bookshelf full of books; if you're a pilot, use a plane soaring through the sky; and if you're a lawyer, use the scales of justice in front of city hall. Another option is to add a banner image that represents a lifestyle or hobby, especially one that is connected to your career or industry. Exercise, such as running, swimming, or biking, is popular, but imagery related to any activity you're passionate about, such as volunteering, throwing clay pottery, practicing photography, visiting museums, playing board games, canoeing, sailing, bungee jumping, or skydiving, could also work—the list is endless.

An image that conveys your leadership and position of authority is also appropriate. For many years, pictures of presenting to an audience onstage or montages implying a sense of leadership in the office, out in the field, or at a meeting, were great choices, as they subtly conveyed that this person was worth listening to. With leadership becoming ever more virtual, these images may be less relevant now and in the future. These pictures are still an option, but you're probably better holding off until you decide when, or if, you'll be out there speaking to audiences again—you don't want to show a photo of something that's inconsistent with current realities, no matter the situation.

There are some images we should stay away from. For example, sometimes leaders place corporate branding, like logos, in the banner—it's a bad move. Not only does this feel generic, but people might not even recognize the logo depending on what it is and how you've presented it. Adding text doesn't help either. Text in the banner is often difficult to read, and it's unlikely that your audience will be able to digest, process, and remember these words. Further, if someone's checking your profile on a mobile device, the font will be so small it will be nearly impossible to read, like a three-by-five card stuck to a telephone pole promoting a yard sale. Similarly, on a mobile device, as people scroll down the page, your headshot will move from the left corner of the screen to the middle, covering any words featured in that part of the banner. And though this may go without saying, just like the headshot, make sure the image is also high res (in this case, a minimum of 1600 x 400 pixels) so it appears clean, crisp, and professional.

What's most important to remember is that the image should be more personal and unique than the one provided by LinkedIn. While the abstract default image is innocuous, if you don't update it, the implication is that you're disinterested, don't care about how you're perceived, or unwilling to put in any effort to make your profile less generic. The banner image should therefore be inviting, relevant, and appropriate to your status as a leader.

HEADLINE

The headline—located underneath your headshot and beneath your name at the top of the page—is often mistaken for the job title. But LinkedIn refers to this section as a headline for a specific reason: its purpose is to easily communicate the *value* that you bring to your job or position, and not only name the job or position itself. As a senior leader, you might have the title of vice president, president, CEO, owner, or founder. All these titles are fairly self-contained; you can be the vice president of almost any department without your audience understanding what you actually do and the value you provide.

So instead of a simple job title, the headline adds context and explanation to your position and responsibilities, and it can even give a nod to your professional mission. "Vice-President, Human Services | Delivering success one individual at a time," for example, is a much more descriptive and telling headline than "VP of HR." The headline can be a lofty vision statement or a more direct one, as long as it provides the followers with an opportunity to learn more about you, your experience, and what you could do for them.

There are two approaches to the headline. The first gives little to no focus on the company you work for. This approach is more often taken by individuals who either work for themselves—such as independent contractors or freelancers—or for a company with little brand recognition. Unknown entrepreneurs are better off referring to the problems they're trying to solve, not the name of their fledgling business. If you're developing innovative approaches to capturing solar energy, you don't want the headline to state "Founder, Capture the Rays | Solving the climate crisis," unless your followers are already familiar with your company, Capture the Rays. Otherwise, they'll have no idea what you do and what specific problem you can actually help them solve. This first approach can also be used for individuals who may not be working for a particular company at the time. For example, "Chief Financial Officer | Sound financial leadership for Fortune 100 companies," implies that you have held this role in the past and plan to continue to do so in the future for the same caliber of companies.

If the company you work for has strong brand recognition, the second approach would be best, describing not just what you do, but also who you work for. In tech, the company you represent is as much of your calling card as your name and position. If your headline mentions Microsoft, you automatically have an in with your audience—the brand holds enough weight on its own. Including a company name with brand recognition also helps to ensure you don't get overlooked. This is important in any business-to-business industry, where people tend to first search for a company to help solve their problem and then narrow in on an individual. When potential clients or collaborators research your competitors on LinkedIn and your name pops up as another possible connection, few people will likely pay attention if they can't quickly find or identify who you work for. They might not know your name, but they will know your company, so it's important to have that company name front and center.

ABOUT

The About section, also known as the summary section, is one of the most critical when it comes to identifying yourself and the leader you aspire to be. It should consist of a description that provides a full picture of who you are, with a visionary statement of what you plan to accomplish in your career, how you lead others, and what your followers can expect when they engage with you. This piece of your profile nods to your past, and how you got to where you are today, but mainly remains forward looking. Since it's focused on your aspirations, it's a dynamic section, subject to updates over time—as you progress in your career, this section should progress along with you.

Unfortunately, many leaders use this section to dish out a boiler-plate explanation of where they've worked and what they've done in their previous roles. This section is not the cover letter of your CV or a travel log of work experience, nor should it be thought of as a work summary. Instead, the About section provides an opportunity to tell your audience what motivates you, what values set you apart from other leaders, and why you're in a unique position to help solve your audience's problems. When you write this material, consider a three-part structure—professional, philosophical, and personal—by answering the following questions:

Professional

What do you love about the industry you work for? What problems do your customers have that you can solve? Why do you love working with your clients?

Philosophical

What life lessons have you learned from your experiences? What characteristics do you value? Is there a quote that you live by?

Personal

Where do your personal and professional lives overlap? Are there hobbies that you love? Is there anything you've learned from experiences outside work that you can apply to your business skills?

When answering these questions, revisit your self-assessment from Chapter 1. Then ask yourself: What is your passion? What gets you up in the morning? Why are you good at your job? What have you learned in your career? Keeping the answers in mind when crafting this content will help you create a more personal brand that people can understand, relate to, and be inspired by. To that end, avoid jargon or stereotypical descriptions. Claiming to be a "results-driven executive with a can-do attitude known for getting things done and regularly exceeding expectations," or something similar, is applicable to any executive, and is not all that inspiring.

It probably feels unnatural to communicate in the first person about your accomplishments without falling into a rote laundry list of the certifications you've received or the titles you carry, but just know that you're not alone. Very few of us feel comfortable describing our accomplishments, goals, and values in a way designed to differentiate ourselves from other leaders. With that in mind, take the lessons you've learned in Chapters 1–3, revisit the self-assessment and your big why, and focus in on authentic, unique messaging that will help you stand out and truly connect and engage you with your audience.

Here's a great example of an About section that incorporates these lessons, taken from the LinkedIn profile of Brian Bakstran, at the time of this writing, senior vice president of global marketing at the IT and software company Veeam:

> As an IT Executive, I've had the privilege of leading marketing, sales and business development teams of all sizes. I believe in a relationship-based leadership philosophy, built on 3 key pillars; Authenticity, Trust, and Respect.

1. Authenticity: Be yourself, focus on helping others succeed, communicate often and set clear goals
2. Trust: It is earned everyday through supporting your team, making business decisions in the best interest of the company and taking full responsibility for your own actions.
3. Respect: Create an environment that is inclusive, professional and energizing.

> For me, nothing is more exciting than watching individuals grow professionally, seeing teams collaborate and helping the company over-achieve their targets. Using the 3 pillars above, I have been fortunate enough to lead some great teams who have achieved amazing results.

Brian succinctly explains, with conviction, what he's passionate about, what he believes in as a leader, and how he supports others. He also avoids a number of common potential landmines that could lead to unforeseen negative consequences.

For example, Brian's words speak to a wide audience, not just hiring managers. If he were to use an opening line like, "senior executive with a demonstrated history of exceeding sales quotas," or "aggressive salesperson with twenty-five years of senior leadership experience in the industry, with proven ability to discover new accounts and consistently expand revenue," it's likely that his customers, and employees, would be turned off. The customer is not going to be excited about "aggressive sales" or "exceeding quotas"—these terms imply that *the customer is* the product. Such statements feel tailored for, and directed at, recruiters. Remember, your profile is *not* an online résumé. If it becomes a résumé, it would imply that you're looking for a job, which means you're no longer doing business, and you're no longer using LinkedIn as a communication and leadership tool.

Another word to the wise, specifically to leaders like myself who have been around for a while: Though "twenty-five years in the business" sounds impressive, it also sounds, well, old. Say it was 1920—the jazz age, the roaring twenties, cars whipping up and down the streets—and then you tell your audience that your work experience goes all the way back to 1895. You're not just talking about a different decade—the gilded age, the gay nineties, horse-drawn buggies plodding up and down unpaved roads—but a different century, world, and way of life. Now apply that idea to 2020. Twenty-five years earlier was a different *millennium*. Some of the people who work for you were barely born in the 1990s. They have no memory of the previous century, so the work experience you're touting doesn't feel relevant. It's tempting to include such material as a quick way to establish your authority and knowledge, but you're better off leaving it out.

EXPERIENCE

Just like the rest of your LinkedIn profile, the Experience section should not be treated as an online résumé. Though it provides information on where you've been in your career, it's not meant to be an exhaustive list of every role you've ever held, particularly those that are no longer applicable to who you are as a leader. Only include positions that relate to what you're doing now and may hint at where you're going in the future. The further you go back in your work experience, the more irrelevant the positions are likely to become, so they hold little intrinsic value for your audience.

If you were a bartender in college but have now been in the tech industry for a decade—or even if you're just entering it—you don't need to reference that job, unless you're either planning on going back to bartending or if it somehow reflects on your position today. Maybe you work for a company that develops apps specifically for service industry workers to better help them manage job-related stress—in that case, it would help to show your customers that you know where they're coming from. Regardless, every piece of content you include in this section should create a visible path to explain who you are, how you got there, and how you're now bringing value to your audience.

The same rule applies to more senior leaders. Just like you shouldn't point out your abundant years of experience in the About section, you shouldn't to do so in this section either. Anyone looking at your profile will know that you have *some* kind of work experience; what they really want to see is how it's applicable and relevant to what you're doing now. The same can be said for entering "months of employment." You don't need to include the months of your employment for any given year. They don't add any important context, and if you do happen to have any gaps in employment, removing them may help to smooth out that disruption.

The material in this section should also be in tune with the statement you've included in your About section. Your audience should be able to easily see how the jobs you've had, what you've accomplished, and what you're striving toward all connect and form who you are as a leader today, as is outlined in the About section. If the two sections are out of whack, you will seem disingenuous and inauthentic, and you could potentially lose your credibility. When the two are in sync, however, they tell a story of who you are, reflecting your personality and professional philosophy, values, and achievements.

Another important and often overlooked aspect of the Experience section is your current job title. Similar to the profile's headline, this piece should provide more details about the specific, unique value you bring to your leadership position. You may be thinking, "haven't I already done that in the headline?" Yes, but there's a little-known trick here: when someone Googles you and a link to your LinkedIn profile pops up, that position from the Experience section—not from the headline—is what shows in the snippet text. Since that's the case, create a tighter, more condensed version of your profile headline, and use it as your current position in the Experience section.

ACTIVITY

Your activity is the most important aspect of your profile when it comes to building your tribe and increasing your influence. The actions you take will be inspected by your followers to see if they are relative to their lives. They will try to discern if you can truly help them, contribute to the community, and lead them, and others, to success. Your follower's inspection is done through the two types of content you create and share via LinkedIn's activity section. You can write articles, which are long-form pieces of content, and you can create posts, or short-form content. You can also generate content through your engagement with other users, which means liking, commenting on, and sharing their posts.

Articles are usually long-form pieces similar to a blog (more on long-form content in Chapter 5). They are often 500-plus words and are usually meant to be evergreen, not tied to a single event or time, but relevant no matter when someone reads them. The content can have multiple graphics or links—including to references or related content you've produced using other social media tools, such as a video on YouTube or a podcast—and is generally designed to hold a reader's attention for several minutes. Articles have a 40,000-character limit, giving you plenty of virtual real estate to type away.

Posts are much shorter in nature, usually tied to an immediate thought, idea, or event. These, too, are oftentimes accompanied by a video or other links. Posts are limited to 1,300 characters, so they are more succinct than articles. This character limit includes spaces and punctuation, hindering your ability to create any content of significant length. When your audience takes a look at your posts, only the first three lines are visible until they click on the "see more" button, which makes the rest of the content visible. As such, those first three lines must immediately capture your audience with a hook or compelling story. Don't bury the lead or ramble through a long-winded explanation—make those first three lines count.

Each time you create content on LinkedIn, it is pushed out to your LinkedIn network. When you like, comment on, or share others' content, a portion of your network sees that activity in their feed. Your entire network does not see every post or action you make, but only a portion based on LinkedIn's algorithm. If your content is boring and uninformative, then you will receive only a few views, and LinkedIn will further limit viewership by not actively promoting it in others' feeds. If your content is interesting and of value, however, LinkedIn will share it with more of your network. That said, if someone looks up your profile and directly checks out your Activity section, they will see *all* the comments, posts, likes, and articles that make up your activity.

FEATURED

As of 2020, LinkedIn allows you to prominently display your posts, articles, videos, and any other content you'd like, at the forefront of your profile in a dedicated Featured section. Like a carousel, you can rotate material in and out of this section, allowing you to communicate with your audience through content you find valuable at any given time. This dynamic element can also act as a place to store and save static, evergreen material, which you can then reference in other posts. This material may include content that is not typically highly promoted by LinkedIn, but that you want to make available to your current and future audience.

A word of caution: The Featured section can be turned on and off. If it's turned on and you don't know it—which happens more often than you might think—it will automatically be populated with material from your profile, including content you may not want to place so prominently. Maybe you haven't updated your Experience section in a while or you haven't yet removed an article from your Activity section that you feel no longer represents you as a leader— the Featured section may still pick up this content. If this happens, your followers might take a look and get an incorrect impression of what's important to you and what material you most want to draw their attention to. Of course, there's a simple fix—make sure when the Featured section is on that it only includes the content that best represents you.

RECOMMENDATIONS

Your audience isn't always going to take your word at face value. You can claim that you're an excellent leader of multinational, cross-functional teams, but if no one can confirm your success in that area, you may have a harder time proving the truth of this statement. Therefore, you want to make sure that there are at least a few people out there who have said something positive about your capabilities or experience in an easily accessible public setting. The Recommendations section of your profile provides this setting. It also gives you the opportunity to recommend others. What you have said about others gives insights into how you treat people. These words can speak volumes about the type of leader you are, or want to be, reflect who you are, and enhance your reputation. If you just rattle off some quick generic praise, it won't be nearly as impactful as a well-thought-out, insightful, and honest recommendation.

Still, you don't need to spend too much time perfecting this section. Set it up early on in the process of developing your digital presence and use it steadily over time. If the recommendations go back a few years, people will likely have more confidence in you and your leadership. This past reserve of "goodwill" acts as your history, helping you demonstrate consistent behavior. This history also helps remove the impression that you're only getting recommendations because you're actively pursuing a new position. If someone sees that, all of a sudden, you gained five new recommendations in a month, and before that it's been crickets, there will be an imbalance, implying you're only concerned with your online presence now for a specific reason—either you're jumping ship or you just got canned.

To get started, the magic number here is just three. You want to give three recommendations and receive three recommendations. The easiest way to do this is to simply go out and first give recommendations to three people you've worked with in the past and that you highly respect. Make sure these individuals are active social media users. Once they see you've recommended them, they'll likely reach out and do the same for you (this also gives you the chance to reconnect with some members of your network who you may have lost touch with for a while). Do this a few times every year to show you're still relevant and to build your connections with other business leaders.

INTERESTS

The Interests section is another opportunity for your audience to get to know you on both a professional and more personal level. Just like you can use the banner image to imply a certain lifestyle or give a nod to a pastime that is important to you, the interests section rounds out your personality. Here, you can add icons of organizations that you're committed to or respect, companies you appreciate, or causes that are important to you. Doing so aligns you with certain groups, causes, or industries you want others to associate you with. Since that's the case, choose wisely—you don't want to come across as pushing an agenda, nor do you want to look like you've tagged every company, cause, and organization out there with no rhyme or reason. Keep them focused and connected to the real you.

EDUCATION

The Education section is straightforward, but there's one main element to note here: your graduation dates. Don't include them. We all know ageism exists, and most all of us worry about how we'll be perceived based on how old we are. Ageism is such a concern today that, in the US, it's illegal for hiring managers to even ask about age. But if we include our graduation dates in our profile, they don't have to, as the information is right there for them. Though it would be nice to think that your age won't work against you, as a leader, it most definitely will—some people will see you as too young and inexperienced, others will see you as old and out of touch. Don't allow ageism to affect your role; leave your graduation date on your diploma and move on.

SOCIAL MEDIA BEYOND LINKEDIN

Though we need to learn about and use all the "big four" social media communication tools, it's definitely a slow build and a natural evolution, so if you're only currently using one or two platforms—or none—that's okay. As your online presence becomes more robust though, you should at least have an account on each platform and use them to the best of your ability. Sign up for the accounts now, get the basics down, and over time, you'll better understand the tools' nuances and how they can work best for you. LinkedIn will always be the one platform that leaders must pay attention to the most, but the other platforms play their own role in developing your overall digital presence and virtual real estate—especially Twitter.

TWITTER

The conversations taking place on Twitter are rapid fire and short-lived, which means there's a lot of them. These small snippets of content are designed to operate in near real time and generally consist of succinct thoughts and commentary on trending topics, like politics or the industry news of the day. This content is almost ethereal. The conversations are there, but they don't hold a great deal of weight. Normally once a comment is made, the creator and audience quickly move on—the life of a Tweet is typically one hour. Still, this type of engagement is important because it includes you in conversations on a rolling basis and provides you with an outlet to quickly tell a story in the context of what's happening at that moment. You should therefore have an active Twitter account, occasionally posting to stay a part of topical conversations related to your business, industry, and personal–professional brand.

You don't need to spend your life reading Tweets. Instead, by taking a more targeted approach, you can engage a group within your audience. For example, you can use certain Twitter tools, like lists, that help you track individuals you want to pay attention to or be associated with. Lists are curated collections of Twitter accounts you can follow and engage with, while blocking out the rest of your Twitter connections and usage. You can subscribe to other leaders' lists, or you can create your own, which can either be public or private. These lists allow you to filter out the noise so you can focus on those individuals that you most want to pay attention to and attract.

Many people use the platform to engage in informal, back-and-forth conversations that can be monitored and dipped into and out of like you would at a large dinner party or networking event. At a dinner party, you can try to listen to every conversation happening in the room, but it would be impossible to take them all in, so you typically move around from group to group, chatting as you go. On Twitter, too many rapid-fire, back-and-forth Tweets come across as extreme digital noise. Instead of trying to keep up with as many as possible, just like at the party, find a small group, spend a little bit of time with them, and focus on what they're saying. Make a thoughtful contribution to the discussion, then move to the next group. Spend some time with them, and then move to the next group, and so on. That's what Twitter is all about—informal conversing on a minimal basis around targeted topics. As a leader, Twitter provides you with the opportunity to briefly engage in a large swath of activity in a short amount of time.

INSTAGRAM

Instagram is a platform for images and hashtags that tell a visual story with limited text engagement. Though most people use Instagram to post photos of vacations or a particularly exceptional—or particularly unexceptional—meal, this tool is important because it provides a peek into your personality. As a visually driven platform that captures small stories, organizations and corporations often attempt to display a snapshot of their culture through Instagram posts. Whether showing pictures of employees, parties, fundraisers, or events, all these images can come together to give insight into the day-to-day cultural activities of a company.

You should use Instagram to show a small part of your personal side that is applicable to the workplace. Do not, in any way, try to compete with or become an "influencer"—leave that to the socialite celebrities. Instead, use Instagram to display the personal aspects of your business life or other items you would feel comfortable sharing at a work function or a networking event. If you're a gardener, for example, feel free to post photos of the biggest, juiciest heirloom tomato you've ever grown. Instagram also has the added benefit of generally being more "fun;" a place to share playful videos, humorous stories, and informal photos that you wouldn't likely post on LinkedIn.

FACEBOOK

Oftentimes, and mainly with an older demographic, Facebook is a place where private conversations happen among close friends and family. This causes many people, particularly leaders, to be uncomfortable with sharing their Facebook accounts with their fellow employees or the public. This tool is typically used for a much more intimate relationship with a private group of individuals. Nevertheless, you still need a Facebook account to convey some aspect of your personal life. How do you do this without giving up your privacy? With security settings. Make sure your security settings are set to private mode for any private events and milestones. Then place key indicators in public that give people an insight into your personal life as you would with Instagram. Not only can you then post a photo of that perfect heirloom tomato, but you can also include text explanation describing the breed, the conditions in which it was grown, and when you started growing it.

This account is important because when somebody looks you up, they'll look at your LinkedIn for sure, but sometimes when they Google you, they'll first find your Facebook account, and start there. Again, this is what is meant by having virtual real estate. If someone checks out your Facebook page and it's blank, missing your photo, or completely shut down, you've missed an opportunity to wield influence. If you can, however, use your Facebook account to entice your followers, you create an opportunity to build engagement with them. To do this, make sure your Facebook account includes public facing aspects that allow you to convey the story, message, and position you want to take while building your online persona. There's no need for you to hide all of your Facebook activity either. Instead, selectively release content you want your targeted followers to see, and from there, you can direct them to your other accounts, such as LinkedIn. As suggestions, they can always create a public page on Facebook and invite people to "Like" it, or even link their Instagram with Facebook.

CONCLUSION

Even if you've mastered the mechanics of these tools, your efforts will be all for naught if you discard the lessons from Chapters 1–3. You can't just sign up, make the profiles, close your laptop, and then check them out once every six months—that defeats the entire purpose. But by mastering these communication tools and using them consistently, you can engage your employees, peers, customers, and prospects and ensure that they know who you truly are, instead of confusing you with some James Bond-esque character locked away in a Russian prison. Carve out that virtual real estate so your digital presence is vast, not just some scattered info that gets lost in all the digital noise.

Using LinkedIn will actively build your credibility, showing that you are participating in social conversations in a way that relates directly to your business expertise, values, and role. As you progress as a leader, your voice will become easily accessible and known, showing your audience—and anyone else who cares to look—who you are, your personality, and the values you believe. Over time, LinkedIn does the leading and personal–professional branding for you, as your profile and activities on the platform put you in front of your audience and tell your story. But you also need to be present and actively use Twitter, Instagram, and Facebook, all of which provide different opportunities for you to stake your virtual claim, build your online presence, and lead your audience with an authentic voice.

TELL POWERFUL STORIES

AS A SENIOR sales leader of a large multinational company, Mark Weber was responsible for several billion dollars of revenue in his region. He'd been in sales in the tech industry for nearly thirty years, having worked for major corporations such as Hewlett-Packard and Sun Microsystems. He was well-known throughout the industry, but he had little online presence and did not actively use any social media tools. Some of his colleagues encouraged him to explore the possibilities of social media, and specifically LinkedIn's, but just like many other senior leaders led astray by the three myths of social media (discussed in Chapter 1), Mark didn't quite see the point. That, however, would quickly change.

Despite his hesitation, Mark decided to give it a try. He skipped some of the earlier tiny engagements—such as commenting, liking, sharing, and reposting—to focus on defining his voice through a series of articles on how to succeed in sales. With the help of a social media consultant, he began working through his inexperience with writing long-form pieces. Though he started producing his own original content, his earliest articles were somewhat vanilla, focusing on fairly generic topics. The first one he developed and had published online was about customer service, titled, "Lessons From Baseball: 3 Ways To Give The Best Customer Experience." Mark chose the topic because he really liked baseball, and was therefore comfortable writing about it, and it gave his readers some insight into his interests.

Though it was generally a strong piece, it didn't speak to Mark's personal experience and values in a way that would likely cause him to connect with his network on a deeper level. This kind of article had a limited audience: salespeople who liked baseball. There might have been a lot of them out there, and they might have been interested in reading the piece, but it wasn't guaranteed to be shared far and wide. "From Baseball" generated a respectable number of reads, but Mark was hoping for a larger response.

His next article, "Hire A Veteran Today: Here's Why," was more personal, focused on an issue that was important both to him and to a wider potential audience. Mark had hired many veterans through the Military Credentialing and Licensing Task Force, a program set up during the Obama administration that provided skill-specific training to vets, helping them enter industries with high-demand for skilled workers, including IT. He described with emotion the men and women who serve in the military and how they can often be a leader's best asset when it comes to team building. The article did better than the previous one, with nearly 15,000 reads.

Mark began warming up to the idea of writing and posting these articles. A growing audience was seeing his work, and he was getting feedback from customers and employees. He became more comfortable with his voice as he recognized people were interested in what he had to say. During that time, Mark received a major promotion, moving from a regional leader to a global leader and senior vice president with a worldwide team, which extended his responsibilities to a much larger stage. In his new role, he would have thousands of men and women around the world working for him—many of whom he had never met—and customers and partners who had never heard him speak in public. It was intimidating, to say the least.

But Mark had a major advantage when he started this new position—he had already begun building an audience and a body of work that could help him engage with his new employees, customers, and partners. He had yet to produce an article, though, that truly highlighted his values, beliefs, and leadership style. Mark realized he had to tell a compelling story—a bigger story. He needed to mine his experience and meld the personal and professional into a narrative that would have a lasting effect.

In the his next article, "Do You Have The Stomach for A Job In Sales?" Mark decided to discuss why someone should make sales their next career choice. Though this sounds simple enough, the true purpose of this piece was to help Mark's team see what drove his passion. Since he would never get the opportunity to personally meet all his team members throughout the world, this article gave him the chance to connect with them on more than a surface level, so they could get to know Mark through a topic specific to him and his role. The piece was much more than a list of "what it takes to do the job." Mark wanted to open up about what brought him to this point, how and why he started in sales, and why it had been such a fruitful career.

The article developed into a personal essay, a reflection on his life and a recollection of events that had created a major impact on him. In the writing process, it became clear to him that from an early age, he had wanted to be in sales because of his dad. His father had been a salesperson when Mark was growing up, and it had given him a flexible schedule that allowed him to spend quality time with his family. Mark recalled how his father was always able to make it to Mark's little league games, and how that influenced Mark's beliefs in the importance of family. He also recognized that by majoring in engineering in college, he was able to understand and sell complex products and services.

He didn't have to write about his expertise or any predetermined talking points; instead, he looked internally, wrote introspectively, and in the end, created an article about his motivations and vision. The stories he told about his life were woven into his larger story of sales. Yes, there was a bit in there about the reasons anyone should become a salesperson, but the story was essentially about *his* decision to become a salesperson—a single narrative about *Mark*, an intimate look at him as a person and a leader. This was the type of story Mark wanted to be known for, and it proved more powerful than all his other articles combined.

The article was an instant success, generating nearly 100,000 views. His teams shared it continually, using it as a means to introduce their leader to their customers and prospects. Sales recruits even began referencing the article in interviews as a reason for applying to work for the company. In 2015, Mark started Weber Strategies, LLC, a consulting company he continues to run. He also began teaching a course on selling and sales management at the business school of the Catholic University of America, and is now the Chair of the Virginia Tech Leadership Council. To this day, in all his professional endeavors, that article continues to resonate, and Mark still shares it with clients, prospects, and others in his community as a way to introduce who he is, what he believes, and how he leads.

As we master these social media tools, we will graduate from commenting, liking, sharing, and reposting to creating more of our own original content. Though tiny engagements will always play a major role in our social media usage and digital-first leadership, we will want to provide more in-depth commentary on the content we're sharing; develop more long-form content, such as articles and blog posts; and incorporate a wider array of short-form content, including podcasts and videos, into our online presence. The best way to accomplish this step up is through strong narratives. Such material is often not centered around lessons learned, but instead around the very emotional and human element of the story itself. Furthermore, storytelling techniques can be incorporated in any aspect of our social media usage. The About section of LinkedIn, for example, tells a story. The commentary we make on others' content can tell a story. We are all people of stories, we are cultures and societies of narratives, and through them we engage others and lead our tribe—it's no different in the digital world.

HOW STORIES ENGAGE OUR AUDIENCE

Social media is really about storytelling. For example, our big why (discussed in Chapter 2) comes down to the story of our lives, the story of who we are, how we got here, and our resulting values. Finding the stories that reinforce our motivations and values, and then sharing them, is a powerful way to connect with our audience. These stories must be developed not just with data points, but with material about our personal narratives that will resonate with the audience. Understanding and experiencing the act of engaging builds a sense of narrative as well; the regular interaction we have with our audience creates a story in itself—our story as leaders.

Telling stories is therefore much more important than simply posting content. The content we share, and how it reflects on us as leaders, is only as good as the commentary and insight we provide in relation to it. That said, it's important to note that "telling a story" doesn't mean that we need to write a memoir, or even focus solely on long-form content, such as Mark Weber's bylined articles. Our stories can be of any length and crafted using any social media tool. For example, Tom Mendoza, the reluctant digital leader from the Foreword and Chapter 1, once posted a video on LinkedIn of his wife and her pregnant belly being blessed by the Pope. They had gone to the Vatican on an invitation from a friend, and they had the opportunity to meet Pope Francis. When they did, they asked if he could bless their soon-to-be baby. The video clearly showed the Pope as he put his hand on Tom's wife's belly and prayed over her. The Mendozas politely thanked him—and then Pope Francis gave them a *thumbs up*. Whether you're Catholic or not, that's quite the story in itself right there. Tom typically gets 10,000 views or so on each post—this one hit around 500,000. He took an opportunity to share a personal moment that was unique and attention-grabbing, and he didn't need to include a single word of commentary to tell it.

When we use narratives to connect with our colleagues, employees, customers, and the public, we give them the opportunity to latch onto material that is much more substantial than typical "leadership lessons" or a regurgitation of facts and figures. Stories are meant to provide insight into who we are as leaders, but also inspire, excite, or otherwise intrigue people around us, leading to an action and a response. They also better help people remember the point we're trying to get across or the information we're relaying. As we engage through stories, our audience tends to grow, but that depends on how we convey these stories. Much of the power in storytelling comes down to a classic lesson from most Writer's 101 classes: the difference between showing and telling.

SHOWING VERSUS TELLING

The idea of showing versus telling is fundamental when it comes to our stories. Dramatization is key in getting a point across, but we often get too caught up in just "telling" people the story, not showing them and guiding them toward the deeper truths or points within it. Instead of providing our own context, criticism, or commentary, we're more likely to direct audience members to URLs and links—"Go watch this video, it's great!"—leaving it up to them to figure out why we shared them. But this process creates a thin, easily breakable thread between leaders and their audience.

In reality, our followers do not connect with us because of the content we share, but because of what's inside our heads—what we can provide that no one else can. They want *our* perspective, *our* story. They want to know the "whys." Why are we posting that link? Why does that content matter? Why is it important to us, and why do we think they need to see it? Our relationship with our followers develops when they find us interesting, entertaining, or maybe even fascinating. If we prove to them that we can lead them to some type of success, then they'll want to understand why *we* find the content we share interesting, entertaining, or fascinating. We must therefore create a story around the content, using our own words and experiences.

Just like developing our authentic voices, this concept of showing not telling, through which we expose a potentially vulnerable part of who we are, is a hard one for many of us to embrace. True leaders are often selfless, seeking to benefit others, not attract the spotlight. When such leaders are asked to share their stories and demonstrate their humility, the idea can feel almost counterintuitive. Many recognize the necessity in person—at talks, in meetings, during presentations and major announcements—but when it comes to social media, they worry about taking the same approach. This belief stems from the same fear we experience in regard to the Myth #2 of social media (Just a Bunch of Self-Promotion) discussed in Chapter 1. We don't want to come across online as boastful, so we feel more comfortable hiding behind PR, our pre-planned lessons, or our books. But in order for our messages to get out today, we must learn to dramatize, share our narratives, and demonstrate our passion in public on a consistent basis.

Many business leaders who were comfortable giving in-person presentations in the past still have troubles recording videos of themselves and sharing them via social media, even when they recognize the importance of connecting virtually with their audience. Some of these leaders in particular (with whom I have worked), had spent twenty years standing in front of people, teaching, training, explaining, guiding, and inspiring. They made a living being out in front, leading and educating others—it was their career. They had even developed courses on how to become more confident when presenting to executives. They had written a book about self-discovery, on how to take a journey to find our innate talents and then build on those talents. They were extremely comfortable in front of audiences of any size.

I assumed that someone with this experience would have no problem recording their thoughts in front of a camera, explaining their beliefs and values, and pitching their message using a personal narrative. Yet, as we sat down in front of a camera to do so, they confided in me that, in their two decades of doing this type of work, this was their first time to capture their message on video. They were visibly nervous, struggling to do something they had done so often over the years, just without a camera in their face. The plan was to record a three-minute spot to share a few points on their philosophy, their book, and their workshops, but it took over two hours of recording, rerecording, and coaching to capture those few minutes of content.

As we reviewed the video, which I critiqued in real time, they were extremely uncomfortable watching themselves. It occurred to them, and to me, that they had never fully been comfortable with the dramatization of their story in a succinct, straightforward manner. They could speak to large audiences, telling them some brief facts about themselves, but then they'd shift into their pre-planned lessons and rehearsed speeches for the next forty-five minutes. There was nothing inherently wrong with that approach in that context, but now that they were producing more content to post online, they needed to reevaluate. Viewers today are looking for well-crafted, brief stories from leaders that signal their expertise and provide convincing evidence into why their advice should be followed. Without a good story, the impact of the lesson wilts.

Similarly, when it comes to LinkedIn, you shouldn't have to tell your followers what you're good at it; your profile should show them. If you claim to have "excellent communication skills," how do your followers truly know that? What can you show them in your About section that proves your ability to communicate? If the section is a total mess or out-of-date, this obviously doesn't jibe with "excellent communication skills." Or if you state you're able to "lead and inspire teams," where's the proof? Can you show them inspirational leadership through your headline? How about your banner? Customers, partners, colleagues, employees, and every single stakeholder who comes to your profile, they all want a story—and you have to give them a good one.

LONG-FORM CONTENT

Though stories are not exclusive to long-form posts, such as articles and blogs, long-form content should become a part of our digital presence as we graduate from novice social media users to masters. This type of content cannot be explained with 140 characters, one or two images, or a short paragraph of text; it acts as a means of expressing an in-depth idea or thought that then becomes associated with us, helping establish our reputation as leaders and defining our brand. Still, the stories we create, and then post or publish, should not come across as navel-gazing introspection without a concrete point. The narratives must be written to engage our audience and contribute to solving its problems. This format allows us the space to dig deeper, but it's not a license to go off the rails—our narratives must serve a purpose.

There are many means for capturing long-form content, including LinkedIn articles and using the Featured section in LinkedIn (as discussed in Chapter 4). Another effective means of capturing this type of content—and providing a continuous reference to who we are and how we lead—is through bylined articles published online. Though the process can be somewhat demanding, finding a publication to publish your written work creates a connection in the readers' minds between that outlet's brand and yours. This type of endorsement implies that a reputable source finds your content compelling enough to associate themselves with it. The downside, however, is lack of longevity: some of these digital publications disappear over time, taking your content with them. To avoid this issue, you can double publish, first on the company's site, and then on your own LinkedIn profile, referencing back to the previous article as long as it is still available.

The potentially temporary existence of these online publications is one reason personal blogging should still be considered a viable way to share long-form content. Though they've been relegated to the sidelines of social conversations, there was a time not long ago when blogs were big. It seemed like everyone and their parents had one, and they covered every topic under the sun—blogs numbered in the millions. Serving a type of social journaling function, bloggers wrote down thoughts, ideas, and events in their lives, documenting what was important to them. But so much of the content was temporary in nature as well, relevant only to the moment or to a specific event.

It was no surprise then when blogging's popularity began to decline around 2010, due, in part, to the growing popularity of other social media tools. Many people who had been blogging on a regular basis discovered that Facebook posts or Tweets were a much easier means of keeping people updated on what they were thinking and doing. Blogs have therefore become less dominant over time, but if approached properly, they are still a valuable resource. Instead of sharing our up-to-the-minute thoughts, we can post long-form content in a blog the same way we can on LinkedIn—creating a place to capture material that has true lasting power and helps define us. Blogs—whether sent out as a newsletter, hosted on a dedicated site, posted directly to LinkedIn, or some combination of all three—can contribute to our long-term brand building.

Long-form content should therefore not be treated as food in the back of our refrigerators, prone to rot—instead, it should have a long shelf life. When we present narratives that focus on universal concepts or big ideas that help define our positions and who we are, we're building our reputations. We must develop content that we'll want to be known for over a long period of time, and that *could* stay relevant over a long period of time, resonating for years and with audiences to come. No matter what the long-form stories we tell discuss, whether how to effectively lead a global team during a time of crisis, or how to negotiate a labor contract, we need them to be as evergreen as possible.

We can accelerate our efforts by creating an impression of a larger, long-term platform via multiple long-form articles on LinkedIn. If we write and post a number of articles—say ten to fifteen—in a short amount of time, this backlog of content further establishes our presence as legitimate. If we place them in our Featured section, when community members visit our LinkedIn profiles, they will be able to easily find a collection of pieces—not just one or two articles—that have a timeless quality and provide a sense of our leadership. Since evergreen content should be relevant no matter when it's viewed, this approach gives our digital presence a more long-term feel.

Then, when we make our voice heard through tiny engagements, we can always link back to relevant articles stored in our LinkedIn profile. By doing so, we further establish our position as an authority on a subject or idea that we want to regularly discuss and engage followers around. When we can point out our experience and familiarity with the topics being discussed in social conversations, our voice is seen as a legitimate one. With an evergreen story, we can also highlight one of these articles every so often, when appropriate. For example, if there's a particular time of year, every year, when a topic comes up—let's say taxes in the spring—and we've written an article on it, we can refer to it in a quick post or rotate it into our Featured section (as discussed in Chapter 4). An article we've produced years earlier can continue to do the work for us. Over time, we will have developed this collection that includes referenceable points on an ongoing basis, allowing our brand to maintain longevity.

PODCASTS AND SHORT-FORM VIDEOS

Podcasts and short-form videos are another powerful alternate means of communicating our narratives and telling our stories. Just like with long-form content, they give us an opportunity to go beyond tiny engagements and produce substantial original content that is all our own. Though podcasts and videos do not always fall under the long-form designation, they can still play a major role in capturing our evergreen ideas as an authority on a subject. Podcasts and videos also have visual and auditory benefits that less dynamic social media tools lack. With the growing popularity of podcasts, for example, we have another opportunity to meet our audiences where they already are. Back in 2004, Apple first offered around 3,000 podcasts for free on iTunes—as of 2019, there were over 800,000 active podcasts available worldwide, consisting of 54 million episodes.[30] During the first half of 2020, over 55 percent of the US population had listened to a podcast, with over 155 million listening to a podcast every week.[31]

Though these numbers sound as if they're likely to produce a lot of digital noise, you can take steps to establish yourself and stand out when you first start podcasting. Of course, a cohesive story must be present, and just like with all other social media tools, you should be striving to speak with authenticity, set yourself apart, contribute to your tribe, and build your brand as a leader. But there's also a helpful "trick" you can employ that's similar to developing a collection of articles to store on LinkedIn.

Most people judge podcasts based on the number of episodes that have been produced—the lower the number, the less likely potential listeners will "tune in." The higher the count, the more validity the podcast seems to have, and the more likely a potential audience member will become an *actual* audience member. So, if you were to put out a podcast and link to it on your LinkedIn profile, you'd want to start by building up a reserve of episodes early on, say five per week, and push yourself to get to one hundred episodes as quickly as possible. Once you get there you can slow down to a

---

30 Brad Adgate, "Podcasting Is Going Mainstream," *Forbes*, November 18, 2019, https://www.forbes.com/sites/bradadgate/2019/11/18/podcasting-is-going-mainstream/#7df1bc4b1699

31 "Why are Podcasts so Popular in 2020," Brandastic.com, June 24, 2020, https://brandastic.com/blog/why-are-podcasts-so-popular/.

more manageable pace, say three times a week, then maybe once a week. At that point, when new listeners come to check out your podcast, they'll see that you have one hundred episodes in the can, which would imply by your current once-a-week production rate that you've been recording and producing the show for almost two years. You can do something similar with YouTube, or other video-sharing platforms, by uploading videos to your private channel, and linking to them when appropriate.

In an interview with Adrienne White, CEO of Fempower Media, she explains the important role that podcasts can play in growing a professional brand:

> Podcasting is an incredibly powerful tool for business owners because you're able to build the know, like, and trust factors with your listeners very quickly. You can strategize your content to establish yourself as the go-to authority in your industry while also aligning your episode topics around your current and upcoming business offers. When you provide consistent and valuable podcast content that solves a problem for your audience, it is very likely that you will increase your awareness pool of potential customers and drive up your business revenue.[32]

Producing such material is part of the long game of developing and sharing evergreen content. Producing a video or podcast dissecting the details of a specific technology or a particular flash-in-the-pan event is not something that ages well—technology changes and events are forgotten. Instead, evergreen is the name of the game. Topics like problem-solving, mentoring, time-management, or artistic talent don't change much over time and remain universal and long-lasting in their importance.

32 Adrienne White, interview by Richard Bliss, December 12, 2020.

It's also necessary to recognize today's realities when it comes to the mediums we're working with. All the social media tools discussed so far are replacing traditional media. In the meantime, podcasts are replacing radio, and streaming videos online are replacing TV. Leaders are much more likely to create genuine engagements online than through these traditional marketing mediums (as discussed in Chapter 1). While these mediums continue to serve a function, their ability to influence and sway opinion into action is small compared to the impact social media can create through strong storytelling and narratives.

For example, in April 2013, four days after the Boston Marathon bombings, David Henneberry stepped outside his home in Watertown, Massachusetts to have a cigarette.[33] Like everyone else in the neighborhood, he'd been warned to stay inside by the police officers searching the area for one of the two remaining suspects of the attack (the first had died in a shootout earlier that day). There was likely no harm in a quick smoke, but little did Henneberry realize that when he went to light up, he'd become part of the history of the bombings and the subsequent manhunt. He noticed a cut strap on the covering of his boat in his driveway, and when he went to investigate, he found a pool of blood and what he thought was the shape of a body inside.[34] He called the police and they arrived shortly thereafter, followed by news cameras and reporters.

Like many others keeping tabs on the manhunt, I watched the news of the capture of the second suspect, Dzhokar Tsarnaev, who

---

33 Ginger Adams Otis, Joseph Stepansky, Chelsia Rose Marcius, Mark Morales, Daniel Beekman, and Larry McShane, "Boston Marathon fugitive Dzhokar Tsarnaev caught after harrowing 22-hour chase," *New York Daily News*, March 23, 2015 (updated), https://www.nydailynews.com/news/national/manhunt-boston-marathon-bomber-suspect-underway-article-1.1321605.

34 Ginger Adams Otis, Joseph Stepansky, Chelsia Rose Marcius, Mark Morales, Daniel Beekman, and Larry McShane, "Boston Marathon fugitive Dzhokar Tsarnaev caught after harrowing 22-hour chase."

would later be convicted and sentenced to life in prison. It turned out that he had been, indeed, hiding in Henneberry's boat, which was damaged during Tsarnaev's apprehension and arrest. As Henneberry's stepson Robert Duffy stated, "I heard they put a couple rounds through his boat. He's not going to like that."[35]

I realized that there was probably going to be a problem for Henneberry in collecting insurance money to fix or replace his boat, considering the highly atypical situation he was in, so I decided to see if I could be of help. I recorded a short video and posted it on a popular crowdfunding platform in an attempt to raise $50,000 to replace the boat. I made the video on the spur of the moment and loaded it on a Saturday evening. Then I Tweeted my video and crowdfunding campaign to the *Good Morning America* Twitter account. I didn't think much of it as I went out to dinner that night, but by the time I returned, *GMA* had replied, asking for permission to use my video on their show. I of course said yes.

The next morning, during the Sunday broadcast, I was thrilled to see my video included as one of the main stories of the day. *Good Morning America* clearly identified my name, my website, the campaign, and what I was attempting to do for Henneberry. Because of that coverage, the local NBC affiliate station came to my home and ran a piece on my podcasting and crowdfunding efforts to raise money for the cause. The story ran multiple times all week, and I heard from friends and family members who were excited to let me know they had seen my story on the local news. It seemed inevitable that the power of television as a mass media tool was getting the story out, and that I'd have the money raised and ready to deliver to Henneberry in mere days.

---

35 Ginger Adams Otis, Joseph Stepansky, Chelsia Rose Marcius, Mark Morales, Daniel Beekman, and Larry McShane, "Boston Marathon fugitive Dzhokar Tsarnaev caught after harrowing 22-hour chase."

At the same time, an online campaign not connected to mine also began raising money for Henneberry and his boat. This campaign was launched through an early online crowdfunding site, Crowdtilt, and promoted by individual users through Facebook.[36] These efforts did not have any news coverage nor any television cameras, and they certainly did not have a national audience supported by *GMA*. I had the support of mainstream media outlets; the other campaign was solely supported through social media communication tools. These two efforts, identical in their goal—to raise $50,000 for Henneberry's boat—took two different approaches and had very different results.

My result, with national television coverage and extensive local coverage generated less than $1,500, which was almost all from people in my immediate circle of friends. The campaign launched via Crowdtilt, however, was able to leverage the power of social media to extend the message far beyond any immediate circle of friends and raise enough money for Henneberry to replace his boat—all $50,000. The campaign was able to generate a message that could easily be shared and digested online; its impact proved to be much greater than any news story on TV. And keep in mind, this was back in 2013—social media tools have come a long way since then, further eclipsing traditional communication tools.

The difference is in the gulf between seeing and reacting. When we watch a news program and see a story that interests us and we want more information, we have to take several actions at that moment. We have to stop the program, find a pen, and write down the information we want to remember. Or we stop the program, grab our smartphones, and look up the material that interests us. Both

---

36 Bloomberg News, "This guy's boat was destroyed in a Boston police firefight. Now the internet wants to buy him a new one," *The National Post*, April 23, 2013, https://nationalpost.com/news/this-guys-boat-was-destroyed-after-the-suspected-boston-bomber-hid-in-it-now-the-internet-wants-to-buy-him-a-new-one.

cases require us to interrupt our activity, take up another action, then return to watching TV. Then we still have to remember after our TV show is over, to go back to our notes, go to our computer or mobile device, and actually look up whatever story we found so fascinating.

In contrast, when our followers see a short, intriguing story via a video we've produced and posted to our social media platforms, any action that we hope them to take can be done then and there. If we provide an additional link—like one that could take them to articles or other long-form content we've posted on LinkedIn—we're able to keep their attention and lead them to a direct action. Or if they are given the ability to leave comments and connect with us directly, we begin engaging with them without any lag time. Of course, engagement is contingent on the power of the story we tell in the video we've recorded, the podcast we've created, the article we've written, or even the commentary we've provided.

CONCLUSION

Even though we are collectively a people of stories, writing our own can still be intimidating. But when we start to develop narratives that share our passions and values, we increase our legitimacy. Long-form evergreen content—including tools we often think less of as "social media," such as YouTube videos and podcasts—provides an excellent opportunity for us to dig deeper, and explore who we are as leaders and how we got there. We can use LinkedIn to support all these endeavors, as it offers a place to store this content and link to it later through the other big three social media tools. We can also include blogs, whether housed there or elsewhere, as they are still a powerful form of social media and an excellent way to experiment with, and publish, long-form content.

When we show, instead of tell, our followers where we're coming from, what we believe, and how we can help them solve their problems, we demonstrate our leadership. Powerful stories engage our followers in a way that a number of disconnected actions or posts online never can, no matter the "size" of the engagement. In fact, all social media usage can be seen as crafting an overall story: the story of us as leaders. The topics and ideas we choose to be known for are our themes, the events and causes we support are our plots, and whether we like to admit it or not, our leadership story will one day hit a high point—the climax—before we move on to another chapter of our lives. In the meantime, our unique narratives allow us to share ourselves, to even know ourselves as leaders, and in so doing, enable us to lead. Without these narratives, we'd be lost.

CHAPTER 6

DON'T GO IT ALONE

A NEW CEO was sitting in the audience of a presentation listening to another executive, Dheeraj Pandey, CEO of the software company, Nutanix, as he discussed his plans for his company's future and how these plans would impact the AI industry. It was an excellent talk, and at one point, Dheeraj referenced the social conversations he had participated in online. Out of curiosity, the new CEO Googled Pandey, whose social media accounts quickly popped up. He had an impressive number of followers—14,000 on LinkedIn, along with another 19,000 on Twitter. Many of the ideas he touched upon during the presentation were echoed through his content and interactions on LinkedIn and Twitter, extending the conversation far beyond the stage where he was currently speaking, and signaling that this was more than just a single speech—it was part of his overall brand. The CEO wondered how the speaker could do all of this on his own.

Then, the new CEO looked themselves up. On LinkedIn, they only had a few hundred connections; Facebook and Twitter weren't any better. They had been in the industry for decades and had a wide network around the globe and across multiple industries. Yet if someone were to Google them, that experience and network would not be reflected in their digital presence. Online, they barely existed, unconnected to the greater ecosystem of conversations and engagement taking place. They decided it was time for a serious change. Just like Pandey, they wanted to ensure they had a relevant voice and the ability to share their vision for the future of the company far and wide. And it wasn't a moment too soon.

Once they started paying attention to LinkedIn and Twitter, they found that even though they hadn't been active on social media, people were out there talking about them. In one case, a prominent journalist called them out for their approach to a product announcement, saying the CEO had "phoned it in" and that they could "do better than that." The CEO was shocked and a bit confused that they hadn't seen the post, or at least been made aware of it. They had been unable to respond to a major industry pundit's critique because they didn't even know it existed, something they had assumed their team would be on top of. But at that time, neither they nor their immediate team had been paying attention to the nuances of the online community, and they had failed to see the issue.

After speaking with an outside consultant, the CEO began working closely with a team within the company that had been specifically created to support their social media efforts. Together, they developed a system to better track these types of social conversations, which helped the CEO take part in them. The resulting interactions reflected positively on both the CEO and the company overall. The CEO also reached out to a set of journalists, including the one who had called them out, ensuring they could begin building a personal relationship beyond a press release or briefing. This wasn't an attempt to "play favorites" or manipulate influential individuals, it was a genuine effort to connect with their audience, including the media, so they had the ability to engage with it first-hand. Going forward, these journalists had direct access to the CEO.

Shortly after, the CEO's company had a data breach that was big enough to make international news. It was reported that hundreds of millions of people's sensitive information had been hacked. Tens of thousands of customers and employees witnessed the disaster, and competitors pounced, attempting to exploit the bad press being heaped on the company. In reality, the number of people's accounts and the nature of the information hacked had been wildly exaggerated in the press, but the damage had been done. Luckily, the company had a powerful weapon to combat the bad publicity: the authentic voice of the CEO, who's online audience now measured in the thousands.

Though the company put together a standard press release, the CEO consulted their social media team, then posted a series of tweets explaining what had happened. Next, he communicated directly with the audience using follow-up tweets, responding to questions and comments by journalists and the public alike. He explained to them the measures being taken to address the breach. Lastly, in a rare moment of vulnerability, the CEO gave a post-mortem explanation of what they had discovered and why the breach had taken place. All this communication online came from them, in their own words—they had a voice and they used it.

The CEO was able to shift the conversation to explain how their company was handling the situation in a clear and accessible way. Rather than allow the competitors and detractors to run free with half-truths, misinformation, and conjecture, the CEO took ownership of the narrative and held the attention of the industry. Within a matter of days, the discussion was over, and the industry moved on without any serious repercussions to the company. Many journalists privately reached out to the CEO in appreciation for the open and immediate response to their questions. The CEO had been part of the conversation, was known to them, and used the trust they had built up to avert a crisis.

This situation could have never been handled with such care, immediacy, and attention without, first, getting online, and second, working with the support of a team. As leaders, we must recognize that, in any organization, the team we lead carries a power that goes far beyond ours alone. Working with a dedicated person or group to help us in our social media efforts increases our ability to stay on message and directly communicate our thoughts and ideas. By creating a coordinated strategic vision with a team, not only do we increase our capabilities of making an impact on our audience, but we also have people to look to for guidance when we run into roadblocks. As all good leaders recognize, we can't go it alone.

COORDINATED STRATEGIC VISION

Strategy is the use of logic and imagination to foresee the results of an action and to deploy finite resources to achieve those results. When it comes to our digital presence, strategic vision is how we can, through logic and imagination, visualize our voice as it fits into the overall mix of online social conversations. It's also how we plan to engage with our audience, using our finite resources to get there. Armed with our self-assessment and an understanding of our big why, we've already begun developing our strategic vision, but further outside input plays a necessary role in a holistic approach to using social media tools and building our online presence.

Many of the principles and advice leading up to this point, may have given the implication that our social media and online engagement is a solo endeavor. But this can't be farther from the truth, particularly when working within the confines of an organization. To best coordinate our strategic vision and social media efforts, we'll need help in the form of a dedicated team or consultant. Think about it: we require others' input when we develop our big why; we can use programs to automate our posts and organize content we want to share; and we're using communication and leadership tools on these social media platforms that we, of course, haven't created ourselves. The point is, we truly never succeed on our own, and with social media, just as with so many aspects of life, to be successful, we need a team.

Whatever the size of an organization, its leaders are always busy. That's why leaders, especially executives, have support in many different areas—social media should be no different. None of us have enough time to do everything demanded of us. Though the seven-minute rule (discussed in Chapter 1) holds true, we need to temper our expectations as we continue to grow our presence. Familiarizing ourselves with social media tools, and then mastering them, will still take time and energy, but having a helping hand— or hands—can get us up to speed faster. This requires a dedicated group of individuals who are in a position to educate and support us. They can enhance the transition into digital-first leadership by assisting with the physical actions of using these tools, at times posting content on behalf of the executive, monitoring responses, and acting as the eyes and ears for the leader. By working closely with the leader, they can provide support in strategizing commentary and posts to stay in line with the vision of the company. Developing a strategic vision together provides guidance on what, when, and how to post. This team becomes a critical extension of the leader's online presence.

BUILDING THE TEAM

Your social media team can consist of a wide range of people based on the size and type of the organization you lead. There is also always the option of hiring outside consultants or assistants who specialize in social media engagement and building digital presence. Or you can do both: bringing outside experts to work with the dedicated teams already in your organization. For a small family-run business, the team can be as simple as a few family members and friends who are familiar with social media tools and are willing to help you. For a medium-sized business, you could call upon younger staff members who are probably the most fluent in online digital communications. When it comes to large companies, though, you should pull in individuals from four different areas, collectively known as "the quad."

The Quad

For a C-Suite leader of a large multinational organization, the quad structure is one of the most effective. It builds on the strengths of existing employees from the following four teams: the corporate social media team, the corporate communications or PR team, the executive communications team, and the sales team. All these teams have duties related to social interaction with your audience (both internal and external), social selling, and the overall presence of the organization and its leaders. As such, they are the best situated to help you develop a strategic vision and increase your online presence.

The corporate social media team drives online social conversations around the company's brand. This means they're in charge of the corporate LinkedIn page, blogs, Twitter account, Instagram account, and any other social media representing the organization. Using these tools, they help tell the corporate story, focusing on announcing product releases, crafting the company's messaging, and building brand awareness online. They are obviously well versed in social media, and their comfort and ease with these tools, and experience running online campaigns, make them valuable assets to your dedicated social media team. Though they may not be used to supporting individual leaders in building their digital presence, they know the ins and outs of the tools and they understand the greater social media atmosphere.

Corporate communications or PR teams have become more involved in social media in recent years. This means their duties may overlap with those of the corporate social media team at times, but they still hold a unique role. Like the corporate social media team, they also help tell the corporate story, but they have an ability to spread certain messages through more traditional avenues outside of social media, such as print or television. This means they target communication with the press or industry analysts, not the general public. They can help you spread certain messages from the corporate perspective, relying on connections only they can bring to your aid.

The executive communications team focuses less on the corporate story and more on your story. They have insights that the social media and communications teams lack, since they are more likely to work closely with you in developing your all-around public persona. They are also the ones who have likely helped you bring out your authentic voice when speaking outside of soundbites and press releases, and who have helped you prepare for media appearances and public events. Such team members best understand how you should present yourself as the leader you want to be known for, while also making sure the values and beliefs you share online align with the values and beliefs of the wider company.

The fourth pillar of the quad is the sales team. Unlike the other three teams, they're not part of communications or PR, but they are an invaluable asset. Leaders' voices—yours included—are some of the most powerful in the sales process. When your voice comes across as authentic, and members of your audience engage with that voice, they feel as if they are getting direct access to the decision maker. They feel comfort in knowing that they are buying a product or service from a real person who is actively working to meet their wants or needs and solve the issues they face. When sales teams harness their leaders' voice, they are better positioned to make a sale—they know what will inspire their clients or customers to action based on your engagement. As such, when you strategically align your social media activities and digital presence with your sales team, you increase the likelihood of their, and your, success.

When members of these four groups come together, working with you at the center, you can begin creating a full-on strategic approach, boosting your personal message, story, and engagement. Each member of the quad brings something different to the table, whether that's support in using the actual tools, help in developing outward messaging, an ability to craft content specific to you, or the knowledge necessary for aligning messages to create sales. Having members from each one of these teams as part of your social media team will be a lifesaver. That said, the quad doesn't come without its own challenges.

Quad Challenges

Each member on your social media team is still part of one of the four teams discussed—corporate social media, corporate communications, executive communications, and sales—so not only may their attention be divided, but they may also have somewhat divergent goals. Each one of these four entities has a different focus, meaning they have concurrent, contrasting needs and desired outcomes, and each individual within the quad follows suit. Therefore, the very team that has been set up to support you may have other objectives than the ones you're trying to accomplish. For example, the corporate social media team is not usually concerned with the individual activities of executives, unless they serve the needs of the corporate team. Therefore, this team might only focus on developing narratives that speak to the corporate brand. The same applies for the corporate communications team members as well.

In some organizations, PR teams want to own all narratives going out to the public since traditionally they've been the conduit for such communication; but PR teams don't always understand how best to use social media tools. They often think of social media as just another bullhorn to shout out marketing messages, not as a way to create dialogue and engagement. At times, when PR teams help leaders with their social media efforts, they may focus on "controlling the message." They don't want leaders interacting "out there;" they want them to say something very specific at a certain time, even if it doesn't properly reflect the leader or help them participate in social conversations. As discussed in Chapter 1, they're focused on the big splash model and they have little room for the flexibility that social conversations entail. It's understandable, too—they've put a lot of time and effort into creating a set narrative, and they're concerned that one unscripted statement from an executive could throw it all off.

Another challenge is that a leader's individual social media usage and digital presence won't quite "fit" anywhere corporately, so confusion about the roles of each member of the quad may remain persistent. When someone from the corporate social media team hears "social media," they may think that the whole team initiative should fall under their purview. And when salespeople hear of the concept of "social selling" (discussed in Chapter 7), they tend to think that they should be the ones running the show. Similarly, "executive social media" sounds a lot like it should be controlled by the executive communications team members. As such, when no one knows who "owns" the team, or who "owns" the leader's voice, a struggle may ensue. In reality, you own your authentic voice, and the team is there to support you. This point needs to be made clear early on, as it will be a new concept for many of the team members in this novel set-up.

A final challenge that you may encounter with the quad is openness to using social media tools. Not every member of the quad may be as willing to open themselves up to using these tools, which might hamper your progress. Being comfortable with social media tools is obviously crucial, however, so no matter who you work with, make sure these individuals are proficient in online communications, otherwise they are in no position to advise and support you. Unfortunately, this situation happens often, where the very people who are supposed to be helping are oftentimes as helpless as the leaders they advise. The people who support you must be as willing to take the time to learn the same social media principles as you are.

To overcome these challenges, you must create a strategic vision together with your quad that you can all agree on, keeping your voice at the center. This vision should play out online in a way that establishes your brand and primes your audience so it knows what to expect from you. If the audience is prepared, and when the time comes for you to voice your opinions and engage through social conversations, it wouldn't come as a surprise. But to ensure you stay on task, while keeping the team united for a common goal, it helps to agree with them on some guidelines in an effort to overcome their potentially conflicting opinions. Then, when you do make a post or share content, you actually move the needle, which all good social media engagement should do.

OPERATIONAL GUIDANCE

The team that supports us also makes sure we stay focused on the strategic vision we have set forth; this is where operational guidance comes into play. Operational guidance sets the boundaries around the organization's communication plan. These guidelines ensure that the leader's social media approach works, not just for the benefit of the leader, but also for the company as a whole—a win-win situation that positively enhances our individual personal–professional brand *and* the organization's brand. Without operational guidance, we are likely to end up with several disparate approaches to how we, on one hand, and the company, on the other, carry out branding and engagement, which can undermine our leadership.

To decide the themes you'd like to focus on, revisit the self-assessment once again, but this time, think more specifically about how your values and opinions play into your *company's* stated missions, objectives, and goals. Once you've done so, put together a few statements and ideas, and bring these concepts to your team to discuss. Don't speak to them in platitudes, such as "the customer's always first," and don't try to anticipate what the team would "expect from a leader." That's a waste of time. Instead, be honest and authentic so they understand where you're coming from on a personal level, and can help weave this authentic voice into your messaging, while aligning it with the corporate branding.

In the meantime, listen to the team's thoughts and feedback. It might be hard for us to admit, but deep down we know it's true—not all of our ideas are going to be home runs. Our team should be respectful of our voice and our big why, but we should also take their advice when they tell us it's time to hit the brakes. Typically, when we first start seeing results from our social media engagement and increased digital presence, we get jazzed! This excitement is important, as it will push us on to accomplish more. But we might also find ourselves coming up with ideas that we think are absolute killers, when in reality, they are absolute clunkers. We need our team to be straight with us, to point out when our ideas or posts don't fit with the direction we've agreed to follow. Sometimes we need some tough love from our teams.

Of course, it's hard for people to be critical of their bosses, so you'll have to be the one to initiate the critique. Ask your quad or designated social media team to give their honest opinion about the topics you want to discuss, for example, or the interactions you engage in once you begin. Get steady feedback from other employees throughout the organization as well, and speak with other senior leaders, executives, and colleagues. You don't want to end up building a whole campaign based around one opinion, only to find the majority of the organization thinks you're way off base. And be prepared to occasionally receive criticism telling you that your idea, post, or article is not just outside the strategic vision, or untrue to the values that you profess, but that it's simply and honestly, total nonsense. It happens to the best of us.

It's necessary to embrace criticism to develop a better under-standing of how to use social media tools to help your organization, and yourself. When you've gone through the trouble of setting up platforms, joining conversations, and creating an online presence, you don't want to blow it—so defer to your team's experience. Accept oversight, especially early on, and help your team help you succeed. Sometimes this means you'll need to push yourself, but don't be afraid to let your team push you as well—that's part of why they're there in the first place.

During discussions with your team, useful material will start coming out, and the best will rise to the top. Once you identify your values, make sure they align with the company's before you go any further. They don't need to be the exact same as the organization's stated values, but you'll need to find common ground (and if you can't, as discussed in Chapter 2, maybe it's time to change companies). Draw up a Venn diagram with your team to figure out what topics are of interest to you and what topics the company wants to drive forward. Once that's decided, and as you get more comfortable with your digital voice, you can expand on those topics to discuss issues that are personally more important to you, while keeping them in the realm of the set guidelines. Still, it always helps to have someone you can consult to make sure you stay on point.

You should also be able to rely on the team to help answer your questions about the more technical aspects of the tools. In my experience as a social media coach, leaders love when I make myself available after a training session so they can ask follow-up questions. They think that if they ask one of their junior employees, they'll lose their credibility—they don't want to be seen as the executive asking how to put paper in the copier. But questions are important, even if we think they might be perceived as "dumb." The fact of the matter is that it's lonely at the top. Most leaders want to project confidence and avoid feeling vulnerable, but they need to get comfortable with vulnerability if they're going to be putting their authentic selves out into the public. Part of this comfort comes from a willingness to ask "dumb" questions and learn from the answers. This willingness will set you apart from many other leaders. And it's nothing to be ashamed of—if you're new to social media, you're often going to have questions, and you're going to make mistakes.

When you do make a mistake, you need to have someone, or multiple people, on your team that you can reach out to for a quick fix. This role of the helper will prove to be the most critical in supporting your social media efforts. When you run into a point of friction while using these tools, you might feel like two tectonic plates have just crashed together and a mountain has shot up before you. You may not know what to do and you likely won't have time to research how to fix your mistake or the problem you're facing. This means you'll probably just stop whatever you're doing and move onto something else. But this also means your operational guidelines have fallen off and you are no longer pursuing the strategic vision you have set forth. That same mountain might be nothing but a tiny roadblock for someone who is intimately familiar with these tools, so if you can reach out to such a person in the moment of friction, you can quickly move on.

For example, if you're new to Twitter, and you've just posted a Tweet containing a typo, you might not know how to correct it. First-time users typically don't realize that you can't edit a Tweet, but actually have to delete it and create a new one. Instead of taking the time to figure out the best way to do this, if you have someone you can contact to help you, they can take care of it then and there. Then, once the problem is fixed, they can walk you through the process of resolving this issue if it were to arise again. By initially fixing the problem, they've helped you move on, and by later walking you through the process, they've helped you better learn how to use this tool and avoid future problems.

Having this team as a resource becomes imperative to making sure you're maintaining engagement, and doing so in a way that is appropriate, targeted, and in line with your strategic vision and operational guidelines. To that end, there should also be a dedicated member, or members, of your team who monitor your profiles and alert you to anything that may need your attention or that you may have overlooked. You can even have a team member who suggests appropriate conversations for you to be part of as they come up. But choose wisely—not everyone inside your organization may be pleased with your newfound digital presence or be willing to lend you a helping hand.

DETRACTORS AND DISINTEREST

Not all your colleagues and employees are going to want you out there, "flying free" on social media, nor will everyone be excited to see your influence and voice grow online. Whether they don't understand the importance of social media, or they're plainly envious of the attention you're receiving and the impact you're making— which might happen from time to time—some people within your company will fight against your efforts. This resistance may take a number of forms, but there are three in particular that are common.

Firstly, some may subtly criticize or deemphasize the importance of your social media usage and digital presence. These are the same folks who are likely still struggling with the three myths outlined in Chapter 1. They will dismiss social media altogether, not realizing its significance as a legitimate and powerful communication tool, but assuming instead that it's a way for you to stroke your ego. By this point, you already know this couldn't be farther from the truth, but your detractors don't.

Secondly, depending on the position they're in, some detractors may have the ability to remove resources that could otherwise support you, including your team. When someone else is controlling the company's finances or head count, it can be a real problem if they don't see the necessity in providing you with the support you need. Typically, this happens if there are limited resources or they don't believe the company can afford what they see as an unnecessary luxury.

Thirdly (and potentially the most insidious), other members of the organization may give explicit directions to employees within the company to not provide you with the necessary social media support. This could come from fellow leaders or even direct reports. Unfortunately, this does happen. For instance, some team members may be assigned the task of ensuring that a social media initiative goes forward and then intentionally ignore it, purposely sabotaging the strategic vision. These individuals may believe social media doesn't have a place in traditional corporate communications, so they actually feel empowered to block social media initiatives. Alternately, they may find these initiatives unimportant, so they push them to the side and focus on "business as usual."

Even when almost everyone supports your social media efforts, there's always going to be at least one person who refuses to get on board. It may seem that these detractors are the worst, but in a way, they're the easiest to deal with. In response to these detractors, Hang Black, vice president of Revenue Enablement at Juniper Networks, and author of *Embrace Your Edge*, shared with me in an interview, to "smile, and nod, and then influence around them. And after a while, the cards fall."[37] If you can convince everyone around this one stubborn holdout, that what you're doing is benefiting the company, this person will eventually be left standing alone, the only one in the room arguing, the only one getting in the way. Once they wake up to the fact that you are already pursuing social media and receiving support from others, their resistance and negative attitude becomes insignificant and they will give it up.

No matter what form or level of resistance you come up against, don't let yourself get distracted or duped by the detractors. Continue to look to your team for their support and assurance. Encourage them to let you know when you're going too far—falling into self-indulgence or self-promotion—or if you get off message. Most of the time, your colleagues and teams will be excited to see the results you produce—it's only when they feel like you're spending too much time online and too little time in the "real world" that they'll begin to see your digital transformation as negative.

37 Hang Black, interview by Richard Bliss, December 19, 2020.

You also need to recognize that just because you want a supportive team, this doesn't mean you'll always end up with one. Some employees don't want to take on what they see as additional work, or they don't want to hold the responsibility of owning an initiative. They might also believe in the three social media myths, especially when it comes to Myth #1 (Who's got the time? Not me!) In their case, they simply may not have the time—this type of support is much more time-consuming than the seven-minutes a day you'll start out with. These employees may feel maxed out, and helping their "tech-illiterate" boss (who probably makes triple their salary or more) establish a digital presence may feel like an added burden; it's one more thing they need to heap on their plate of duties.

If your team is not comfortable driving this initiative, then it's up to you. You have to take small incremental steps, identifying where you need to go, and how you're going to get there. You have to lead. So, after designing the strategic vision with a team, for example, you could take more responsibility on yourself, starting with something as simple as setting up a Twitter account, and having just one person monitor what you're doing—maybe even a hire from outside the company. Despite the detractors and disinterested team members, you must have support at one level or another, encouraging you to implement the strategic vision you set, and follow the operational guidance you developed.

CONCLUSION

Don't be scared to ask for help—in fact, recognize that you will. You'll most likely face a sharp learning curve when you begin using social media tools, and you will need support, both technical and strategical. Internal teams or outside assistance will help you follow through on the predetermined strategic vision and operational guidance that you've developed, keeping you on task and making sure your digital presence grows in the desired direction. By working with a helping hand, you further ensure that you develop your presence in a coordinated fashion, so your messaging and conversations stay clear, connected, and beneficial to the company's agenda and vision, while still remaining authentic to the leader and person you are.

Scott Pfeiffer, CEO of Strategy Business Consulting, explains how this concept works:

> Successful leaders rely on their staff to create a detailed battle plan. This plan has three components: strategic vision, operational guidance, and tactical execution. Successful executives and entrepreneurs must approach the use of social media in much the same way:
>
> 1. Set a strategic vision: What is your "why?"
> 2. Establish operational guidance. Operational guidance sets the look, feel, tone, and voice.
> 3. Tactical excellence: None of this matters if you don't execute.[38]

Over time, you will be able to rely less on your team and more on the platform you've built with their help. Still, don't be surprised if not everyone is on board with your digital transformation—be aware of it, adjust to it, and move forward. If you're unable to put a support team together—whether due to a lack of interest or finances—consider hiring outside help. Today, it's incredibly important for digital leaders to weave the human aspects of their personality with the corporate issues they discuss in the context of their roles—that's where strategic alignment is crucial. As such, they will often need help from a team to do this successfully.

---

38 Scott Pfeiffer, interview by Richard Bliss, November 15, 2020.

CHAPTER 7

FOSTER A DIGITAL-FIRST CULTURE

IN THE SUMMER of 2020, an executive whom I had the opportunity to work with came to me with a concern. They'd had a fruitful career and a fulfilling, well-paid job at a company they'd been with for years. But right before the pandemic, the company was purchased by a private equity firm. It had since been heading in a direction that concerned the executive. Looking at the company's dynamics, it seemed like it might be time for them to consider moving onto another role elsewhere. Still, they recognized the realities of the economy and the job market—with mass layoffs and closing businesses, it didn't feel like the right time to make any drastic career moves. Or so they thought.

Many companies that have been able to weather the storm and navigate the nightmare of the pandemic are still struggling. Those struggles, however, are not limited to economic uncertainties brought on by Covid-19; they also extend to the inability of old skill sets to meet new realities. Many leaders are uncertain of what to do: They can't travel anymore. They can't bring their employees together for large company meetings. They can't hold big events or attend industry-wide conferences. They're at a loss, and this executive felt the same. They wondered, what's there to do, and how do we lead, in a world that feels as if it's been turned upside down?

What this executive didn't let themselves acknowledge, however, was that they actually had the right background for this exact moment. As the vice president of a worldwide marketing firm, they'd already been working for a company that was almost completely remote. Their teams were spread all around the world, and though they had some regional offices, many of the team members regularly worked from home even before the pandemic. This meant the company had an entrenched digital workflow, and the executive had an established command of the necessary online communication tools, from LinkedIn to Twitter, and from Zoom to Slack.

Though this crisis was not inevitable, this executive's skill set had been developed to meet such formidable challenges, whereas many others' had not. They had a digital-first leader advantage, and through this advantage, they were able to successfully maneuver the company over the first four months of the pandemic. The company continued hiring, training, and doing business. With their mastery of social media and online communication, this executive was already primed for this type of business-altering event. Through our conversation, they realized that if they left their current company, they would still thrive in a new organization because they would bring a value that many executives currently couldn't, that is, the ability to lead in the digital world.

If they made such a transition during the pandemic upheaval, companies were going to swoop them up, because they would be coming from a truly digital-first leadership culture fostered by a company at the forefront of this changing world. They would succeed with their digital leadership skills because they had been developed in a business culture that supported them. They just needed to change the way they thought about the skills necessary to be a leader in today's environment, which were far from the same they were a few years, or even a few months, earlier. That realization alone gave the executive the confidence to move forward.

Leading in a virtual environment is new for many of us, but as it further becomes the norm, we need to recognize, just as this executive did, what skills we have and which ones we need to develop and hone to succeed. This concept is still so new that finding a seasoned executive who already grasps it when coming into an organization is very hard. Not many leaders are building their online presence and participating in social conversations, and if they are, they may not be doing it properly. Very few of them can demonstrate a comprehensive ability to develop their voice and engage with others online. Those who can, and who possess the ability to leverage their current platforms and presence once they move to a new organization, or assume a new role, are increasingly more desirable.

Our digital presence doesn't imply a substitute for a real-world connection—instead, it *creates* that real-world connection, giving us the ability to lead no matter the circumstances. Though we can never replace the intimacy of in-person interaction, we can replicate its results. Using these tools and methods, we can embrace a new way of leading our teams and fulfilling our audience's wants and needs. If we alone, however, take the initiative and no one else follows, our business cannot thrive. To that end, we must foster a new business culture, focused on our vast digital and online capabilities among today's realities.

SOCIAL SELLING FROM THE C-SUITE

Gail Mercer-MacKay, founder and CEO of Mercer-MacKay Solutions, a content-based marketing firm (and the company that developed the Mercer-MacKay Digital Executive Program, mentioned in Chapter 1), learned the importance of digital presence when she started the company in 2007. When she Googled herself at that time, her name only popped up once or twice, while a UK-based law firm, called Mercer-MacKay, dominated the search results. Fast forward to 2021, this is no longer the case. Since 2007, Gail has been increasing her online presence by leaps and bounds. If you Google her today, you'll see her name on the first *ten pages* of results. She got there by consistently sharing intriguing content online on a regular basis, so her audience members knew what she stood for and could easily understand what she could do for them.

But her story is not just one of creating presence, it's of what that presence can do for the company she runs. What she hadn't realized when she undertook her social media makeover was that her presence would actually sell for her while she slept. For example, after she began building her presence, she got a call one day from a potential client. Though she had never heard of the company, or the person at the other end of the phone, she agreed to come into their office for a meeting. She prepared as she would for any other such event, walking through her deck and going over her sales pitch. Gail expected that when she arrived, she'd run through her spiel, at which point the potential client would say, as they typically do, "Thank you very much. We have two other quotes we're reviewing, so we'll get back to you when we've made our decision." This time was different.

When Gail arrived at the company's office, she was shown to a boardroom. As she walked in, she found a woman sitting at a long table, waiting, apparently, for her. Before Gail had the chance to even exchange any basic introductions or pleasantries, this woman's eyes lit up with excitement. She hopped out of her chair, ran toward Gail, and physically embraced her in a near-bear hug. She said to Gail, "I can't believe I'm meeting you. I've read all your blogs. I follow you on LinkedIn. I follow you on Twitter. I know you can help us. I've got money. Let's get started. Tell me what you can do!" They started working together that day. It was the shortest sales cycle of Gail's life, lasting only thirty seconds.

Gail's story illustrates what I like to call "social selling from the C-Suite." This is a process in which an executive's, or other leader's, social media engagement leads to direct sales, addition of new clients, or other quantifiable business results. As digital-first leaders, we are in a unique position to affect how the organization we work for or run engages with consumers and sells our products and services. We invite individual customers to interact with us directly, to pull us into conversations and topics that they, and we, care about. Instead of attempting to connect with some faceless corporation, we can work with others to help them find solutions to their problems and improve their day-to-day lives. When we open ourselves up, making ourselves accessible and available, we encourage a type of collaboration. In so doing, we lead the discussions around the business we can do together. Our audiences are much more likely to accept us as authentic, and let us help and lead them, than try to engage with a brand logo.

In the past, this may not have always been true, as leaders did not yet have the tools to directly engage with their audience. And even today, as mentioned throughout the book, few leaders actually use these tools, though they are now available, because they don't know how. Throughout their careers, they have had little exposure to, and use of, social media as a professional communication tool. Since so many are ignorant of these tools, members of the social media corporate communication and PR teams in larger companies, for instance, fear letting go and allowing their executives to partake in social media initiatives on any deeper level (as was touched on in Chapter 6).

They see individual leaders' social media use and digital presence as almost separate from the company's operations and culture and therefore believe the brand name alone can have a better reach. Traditionally, that may have been the case, but once leaders begin to use these tools on a regular basis, that entire equation gets flipped on its head. Executives actually have a huge advantage over the corporate brand when it comes to building a relationship with the audience through social media. Yes, as discussed in Chapter 4, company name is important to our position and status as leaders, and that's why we'll want to make it prominent on our LinkedIn profile. But, once that's established, we are able to create a much higher level of online engagement with our community and audience than our companies' corporate social media platforms can.

In fact, on average, a post on LinkedIn from a corporate account generates about a two percent viewership, or exposure rate, based on its followers.[39] That means if a corporate profile has a thousand followers on LinkedIn, only about 20 of them will actually see every post the company makes through that outlet. On the other hand, an executive who is active on LinkedIn has a 15 to 16 percent exposure rate.[40] If they have a thousand connections, 150 to 160 followers will see every post they make—up to eight times more than the amount through the corporate page. With those types of numbers, executives and other leaders are better positioned to connect with their target audience and sell to consumers than the brand is able to on its own. A digital-first leadership culture realizes that fact, and,

39 Richard van der Blom, Just Connecting, 2020, Justconnecting.nl.
40 Richard van der Blom, Just Connecting.

in turn, supports its leaders' voices and messages and leverages their unique perspectives, so the leaders' social media strategy becomes part of the company's overall strategy.

When we start engaging directly with the audience, not only are we sharing our voice, but we're supporting the overall organization. As discussed in Chapter 6, sales reps, or any other employee, can point to the content we're creating and posting, giving our current and potential clients and customers insight into who we really are, how we lead, and what that says about the organization we run. Sure, it's easy to share a press release and disclose the company's mission statement, but when others see the interactions we're part of, and the value we're providing as leaders, they're given another reason to trust us with their business. If we're doing our job right and using these tools properly, we will easily prove our authenticity, which invites our audience in. This engagement helps our sales team open doors and close businesses with our clients, which is what this concept of social selling from the C-Suite is all about. When prospective customers know us, they feel more confident in giving our organization their business.

This doesn't mean you should downplay your company's brand; in fact, you can, and should, support and celebrate it. What it does mean is that you have the ability to impact your company's sales directly through the type of engagement you pursue. As the organization recognizes this fact, they are more likely to support you in return. The heart of social selling is the same as the heart of your digital presence and use of social media—you are not pushing out announcements, but actually drawing your audience in. When that happens, your audience recognizes the value you can provide and want to be part of the same conversations you're having. This is not only true for your audience, but also for your employees. They, too, should be inspired to join in these conversations so they can share in where the company is headed, and have their voice heard by you as well. This multiple-way communication—interacting directly with customers, employees, and the public—gives you the chance to highlight individual conversations and pull people, ideas, and concepts into the mix that may have otherwise never been presented.

You're not just "writing posts," you're working with those around you—you're leading. And once everyone within an organization participates at one level or another, the culture begins to respond and change. You would no longer be approaching social media as an individual contributor, but as a team coming together to drive a bigger and better narrative. *That's* how you sell in this day and age—*that's* how you do business. If companies fail to recognize this power, they'll never be able to stay relevant. Regular, old corporate messaging is going to consistently fall flat as companies that embrace digital-first leadership build a thoroughly modern culture, one in which every leader and team member can take part.

ALL HANDS ON DECK

If we demonstrate the strength of social selling through our social media efforts and digital presence, others within the company will want to join in. Before this digital-first approach filters down to employees, though, it must begin spreading across to our colleagues. Other leaders in the organization need to be just as willing to be vulnerable and teachable, taking the time to learn and practice these tools and lessons, while also doing a bit of soul-searching. Through our experience, we'll hopefully inspire other leaders, or maybe they'll even inspire us. If we begin working together on a collective social media approach, the returns will be greater than if we were to develop our online presence separately.

To start, identify other leaders within your organization who you believe will be open to taking this social media journey with you. They may at first be few and far in between, but as you begin to exhibit success through these tools, your pool of volunteers will grow. Once identified, begin coordinating what role each one of you will have in the context of your unified social media message. For example, if you're the CEO, you'd likely discuss trends in the industry, and the company's vision, targets and objectives. The sales leader could focus on the value of the business to the clients. The CTO can cover the tech side of the products and services the company produces, and how they fit into the overall industry and environment. A complex web will start to form, so decisions about who is going to drive which conversation must be made in advance. It is also important to consider which leaders will be called on to respond to a crisis, and which audience they'll be speaking to, whether reporters, customers, employees, or the public.

With multiple leaders developing their digital presence, dedicated teams—like those discussed in Chapter 6—can ensure that leadership stays in tune with one another and supports each other throughout the process. If multiple leaders within a company are seen leading digital conversations through social media communication tools, it reflects well, not just on their leadership skills, but also on the overall organization. To get to that point, however, there must be a calculated approach. Once the roles and conversations are decided upon for each leader, you all need to work together to decide where you're going and what steps you need to get there. In a way, it's about figuring out how you can talk about something without directly talking about it.

You need to develop a way for each leader to strategically "drop breadcrumbs," creating a digital path their audience can follow. When the time comes to announce a new initiative, make a comment on a topic, or otherwise engage the audience, the audience can look back and see that each leader has participated in conversations that may not have felt totally connected at the time, but have clearly come together down the line. These breadcrumbs allow both your individual and collective leadership vision to prep the audience for an inevitable time of crisis or opportunity to which you will all respond.

To get the most out of your coordinated efforts, you can develop specific campaigns tied to particular events or calls to action where these multiple leaders can participate. Take a product launch, for example, as an event in which the three participants mentioned above—the CEO, the head of sales, and the CTO, can play a part. Create a four-week schedule leading up to the launch. Use each one of these executives' unique perspectives to tell a slightly different story based on their area of expertise and social media engagement. Start by deciding which one of you will begin the discussion. This decision could be based on the number or type of contacts and followers a leader has, or it could more directly relate to the product being released. The CEO might be an obvious pick to kick off a product launch, as compared to, say, conducting a webinar on new product features after the product has been released, which might be better addressed by the head of sales.

No matter who begins the conversation, you and the rest of the leaders within your organization can now begin to repost, comment on, and engage with that content. Each one of you can pick a different piece of the value proposition to focus on in your posts, telling a slightly different story leading to the upcoming launch. Think about what each of you will contribute and how that will help drive the conversation and engage customers or the public. As the audience begins interacting with you, commenting on your articles on LinkedIn or posts on various platforms, multiple conversations can start taking place, all still focused on the same event. In time, the idea is to get the leaders and employees to play a part, commenting, posting, and targeting a given audience and influencing the desired outcome.

Story arcs covering a specific topic or conversation can also be incredibly effective and can generate a real ROI. Talk to your fellow leaders about the conversations they might want to be part of, or the topics that they feel comfortable discussing. Say you want a certain number of people to sign up for a webinar that is happening in the following week. Or maybe there's an account, or a number of accounts, you're targeting as potential new clients whose business you hope to have by the end of the third quarter. No matter what the event or call to action is, you and your fellow leaders should be cross-referencing the conversations you're having, building that web of interaction. You'll also begin pulling in employees, customers, and partners who have the opportunity to participate. This type of cross-posting will create deeper discussions online and build an environment in-house that is open to, and embraces, this use of social media tools.

This process can become extremely tactical and take some serious coordination, but you'll quickly see results. Whether for specific campaigns or just as a general approach, you'll still need to put in the time and effort to get others to participate. Again, if you're able to first demonstrate how successful you've been in utilizing these tools and building your presence, your argument for their utilization by others will be automatically bolstered. And as other leaders join you, employees and team members will take notice. In time, you'll want this type of social media usage to influence not just your fellow leaders, but the people you lead within the organization.

FILTERING DOWN TO EMPLOYEES

Once leaders recognize the need to instill these ideas in themselves, they'll also recognize the ability and need to instill them in their teams. Then, these leaders—you included—must be able to convince their employees of the power and necessity of these tools going forward. It's not until the employees throughout the company accept these ideas that a culture can truly be built. Though you can direct a culture through setting an example, unless the majority of people within the company actively participate, or at least recognize this approach's importance, that digital-first culture will never take hold.

Of course it's easy to hope that once employees see their leaders using social media in this manner, they will follow in their footsteps, engaging an audience or community through their personal digital presence, benefitting their career and contributing to their company's success. But let's face it—it's not that simple. Though many employees know how to use these communication tools for their own entertainment, like many leaders, most are unfamiliar with how to use them as professional tools for doing business—nor do many of them want to.

Since its inception, social media has mostly been viewed as a personal tool and space. If we are to ask our team members to use that tool and space to promote the company—a concept known as employee advocacy—many will likely feel as if we are overreaching our boundaries. As social media has progressed, almost everyone recognizes anything they post can, and will be, scrutinized, potentially affecting their personal and professional lives. We've seen in the past how companies monitor their workers' social media activity, and we continue to see today how videos of us are easily uploaded online and can go viral in no time—especially when we don't want them to. The last thing any of our employees want is to feel as if

"Big Brother" is watching over them and that they must utilize their own online presence for the betterment of "the brand."

Much of this stigma, however, comes from a time when social media was solely focused on Twitter and Facebook, not on the social conversations enabled by LinkedIn. Though all the platforms play a role in our digital presence, remember that LinkedIn is where we get business done. That's the shift that must be clarified to our employees and team members—we're not asking them to post private photos or push agendas, we're asking them to engage others using the tools that are now central to all communication. And the tool that is most essential for their purposes at work is LinkedIn. When social media started, no one recognized that these tools would become such a main part of the way we interact. That may have caused personal and professional usage to blend at times, but as discussed in Chapter 2, we can, and should, always avoid exposing what we want to keep private.

Think about it—if you're a salesperson, would you give your cell phone number to a client? How about invite them over for a backyard barbecue? If they have a multimillion-dollar account, you probably won't mind telling them to give you a call if they run into a problem or have a question. You might be happy to introduce them to other clients or even professional friends in a small gathering. This blending of personal and professional is nothing new, it's just somewhat harder to adjust to as we're still acclimating to new uses of social media, including employee advocacy.

As such, one of the duties of being a digital-first leader is helping your people through this period of adjustment, so they can strike a balance they're comfortable with and get the most they can out of these tools professionally. It may help to remind them that by participating in social conversations and engaging in a wider atmosphere, they aren't just helping the company, they're also helping themselves build their own personal–professional brand. We must work with our team members and employees to clearly explain that what we expect from them is a level of *comfortable* participation that will actually help them do their work. We need to understand how our employees are currently using social media and then ease them into finding ways to utilize it to help them solve problems, connect with customers or partners, and otherwise meet their goals.

To guide this process, start by reaching out to your employees. For example, rather than wait for individual employees to reach out to you, initiate the request to connect with them on LinkedIn. This is a powerful way, not only to lead by example, but to take the opportunity to directly interact with the people that actually make your organization run—they are the ones that will ultimately decide if your digital-first leadership efforts are worth emulating. When you connect directly with them, you're acknowledging that you "see" them, that you know who they are and that you believe their opinions and participation are important. By making that first connection, you're also breaking an invisible barrier. Many employees are hesitant to take an action they believe will appear intrusive to their bosses, or will imply that they're "sucking up" to them, and initiating these online, social media connections can feel that way. By reaching out to them first, you're putting them at ease and encouraging them to use the social media tools available.

Another option is to help simplify the social media process through employee advocacy software. This software allows a company to provide its employees with preapproved content they can share online. This content can be accessed on the employees' computers or mobile devices, and with the push of a button they are able to post it using their own social media accounts. They don't *have* to, of course, but by somewhat automating the process with such software, you can help your employees to easily and quickly participate in social conversations, supporting both the overall mission and brand of the organization.

Some employees are more likely than others to embrace this social media-centric approach. Those who are more familiar with these tools or use them on a regular basis will probably be more open to the idea. Salespeople, for one, often use LinkedIn as a way to connect with prospective clients, so they may already have some ideas on what type of conversations they'd like to start or participate in. They might actually be the best employees to first connect with when undergoing such an initiative since they fully understand the organization's brand. But they may need some help deciding how they want their voice to fit into the overall digital environment.

To that end, having them perform a self-assessment similar to the one in Chapter 1 will give them an opportunity to explore what they'll want to be known for online. Even better, they may already have a well-established presence. They can be relied upon as examples of the power of social media and online presence within the company, further encouraging other employees to take note and participate. Still, unless you connect with your employees, this culture will never take root. And it's not as simple as just reaching out to them once or providing them with some information and then having them run with it.

PERSPECTIVE AND PATIENCE

In case this all sounds like pie in the sky, it's important to note that this type of culture is already growing. In 2010, if you were to look up the top ten most connected CEOs using social media, most all of them would have been the heads of, you guessed it, social media companies. Nearly ten years later, this list looks drastically different: as of 2019, according to research by CNBC, of the top ten most connected CEOs on social media, *zero* were heads of social media companies.[41] Lynn Good of Duke Energy, Doug McMillon of Walmart, Hans Vestberg of Verizon Communications, Mary Barra of General Motors all made the top ten list—these are bread-and-butter, long-running companies, and their leaders are a far cry from someone like Mark Zuckerberg.

The point is, any leader in any company can help develop this culture, but we must first change the way that we as leaders, and our fellow leaders and employees, approach social media—there will likely need to be a full shift in perspective. For leaders, building a digital presence and creating results through the strategic use of social media tools doesn't happen instantaneously. It therefore shouldn't be a surprise that it will take time for colleagues and employees to embrace this approach as well. And of course, this can be hard. Getting ourselves organized and dedicated is difficult enough; getting one team organized and dedicated is even harder; getting the whole organization on board can feel almost impossible. But it's not. It takes time and patience, the main ingredients for leaders looking to implement any type of systematic change within their organization.

The biggest roadblock to fostering this type of digital-first culture comes in the form of establishing the right behavior. Building positive habits and bringing social media to center stage won't take place without consistent practice. A long-term perspective is absolutely necessary here. Though many people within our organization will be looking for immediate results, incremental improvement should be the goal. To achieve this goal, social media cannot just sit in the back of our minds—it needs to be part of our everyday

---

41 Elizabeth Gravier, "The top 10 most 'connected' CEOS on social media—and where you can follow them," CNBC.com, June 25, 2019, https://www.cnbc.com/2019/06/25/the-10-most-connected-ceos-on-social-media.html.

actions, as discussed in Chapter 1. When it's not, we lose both the confidence and the skills to properly use these tools.

When we don't use social media consistently, it's possible for us to forget best practices and to let our usage taper off. I've seen this happen a number of times after I've done training sessions with executives or salespeople. When I do a training session, the feedback I often receive from the participants at the end of the session is that it was the best social media training they've ever had. And yet, I've gone back to that same company and group a week, two weeks, or even a month later, to find that nothing in the practices of the vast majority of participants has fundamentally changed. I'll sit with the same team and ask, "What happened? What prevented you from implementing the things you learned?" Normally, the answer will be that they had questions and ran into roadblocks. The problem is that putting these concepts into practice is just so new to them. After the training, when they went back to their regular environment and daily routines, they asked themselves, "Now, what did he say about the banner? Where do I begin with this type of engagement? Should I be posting or writing an article or just commenting? How do I do this?"

These new concepts of social selling and digital-first leadership are radical. It's not easy for employees to develop a coordinated approach of long-term thinking, identify an audience, and ease into relationships, all with social media at the center of their efforts. But it's necessary, and oftentimes leaders just don't have that kind of patience. Without actually changing their behavior, however, they won't understand the true power of social media. When multiple leaders lose patience and give up, this trickles down, entirely obliterating the opportunity to build an actual digital-first culture. You can't just tell your people, "Hey, let's kick up our social media game a notch," if you're not fully invested and engaged yourself. You also need to follow up with your team members to make sure they stay on task. Otherwise, they'll go back to relying on whatever has worked previously for them—which could be methods that are beginning to fail in this digital environment.

You need to help participants in your team move beyond these old ways of work and outdated mindsets. Even then, keep in mind there are going to be laggards, people who will be behind everyone else in adopting this technology, or who may just never adjust to these new realities. They may require the most attention, or as your organization's culture progresses, you—or they—might realize that they are no longer the right fit. Though that's never easy, there are times when these realizations are necessary.

In the meantime, to foster this culture, you might have to get creative. In addition to getting multiple leaders to participate, utilizing employee advocacy software, and having teams attend training sessions, some companies have found success in social media "selling days". These events are like telethon days, where your sales team spends a full day just calling customers. The social media equivalent is when your sales team spends all day commenting, connecting, and engaging with customers through LinkedIn and other tools. This also builds a type of peer pressure to get more people throughout the company to participate, so nearly everyone takes part, allowing the entire company to experience these tools in a concentrated, focused effort.

Of course, this is just one option. Find what you believe will work for your organization and give it a try. As a digital-first leader, you need to understand that the processes your colleagues and employees have used in the past to find success are often no longer sufficient, and if they aren't outdated yet, they will be shortly. You must figure out ways to help them shift their priorities, stay focused, and use these tools, given the unique attributes of your company and industry. Only then can a digital-first culture truly begin to flourish within your organization.

CONCLUSION

Building our own digital presence and mastering social media tools is a feat in itself, so developing a full-on digital-first leadership culture is by no means easy; it takes time, patience, and hard work. But then again, what worthwhile goal doesn't? As leaders, we can influence the environment around us, but it's not until our colleagues and employees embrace these ideas that a culture can truly be developed and supported. We must therefore progress beyond our individual efforts and focus on a team effort. When working with multiple leaders, coordinating posts and content can be extremely complex and tactical, but in time, the entire company can embrace these techniques and work them to their advantage.

Just like the other leaders we work with, some employees will be more averse to these ideas than others. Salespeople are a good group within the organization to target, because many probably use these tools already. Eventually, though, we want to get everyone to participate. Multiple-way communication—interacting with customers, employees, and the public—creates an unprecedented opportunity to highlight individual conversations and pull people, ideas, and concepts into the mix. As we all work together, a culture of support begins to develop. And as leaders, we're not undertaking these efforts for our personal gain only, we're working to create a better organization that can meet modern-day complexities head-on and contribute positively to the world around us. Without a culture working toward this goal, we'll never get there.

CONCLUSION
WHY WE LEAD

IN SETH GODIN'S *Tribes: We Need You to Lead Us*, the author and marketing guru discusses the idea that there are groups of people just waiting for someone to step out and lead them. It's no wonder why as the world continues to face transition, turmoil, and change, businesses, organizations, industries, communities, consumers, audiences, and all tribes, need guidance and support. They require leaders who can help them through challenges and crises, and seize opportunities to move forward, progress, and succeed. Whether you run a small mom-and-pop shop, a multinational conglomerate, or even a country, it takes resolve, determination, and true leadership to overcome the many challenges you face. When Godin wrote his seminal book in 2008, the world was different, and social media tools were still budding. Now, with these tools, you are better positioned than ever before to be one of the few who step out and lead.

Still, social media is only as effective as the leaders using it. It's your vision, values, and voice that allow you to engage and lead others, whether that's through social media tools or on the ground, in-person, in front of an audience. Today, though, online and in-person communication have become one and the same; they can no longer be thought of as separate approaches. How you act, engage, and lead offline influences how you are perceived online, and vice versa. The holistic approach to leadership combines social media tools and your online presence with the decisions you make in real life that affect real people. This is how business takes place, how leadership happens in the real world. These tools allow you to always be communicating, always be engaging, always be leading.

You're now surrounded by a workforce that is increasingly comfortable using modern communication to express themselves, to share ideas and innovations, and work together to solve problems no matter where they are located geographically. These tools aren't just for the young swapping photos and memes, they are an important part of how our society engages in meaningful interaction. If you refuse them, not only do you place yourself at a disadvantage, but you place the people you're attempting to lead at a disadvantage as well. To be a digital-first leader means knowing these tools inside out, mastering them effectively, and using them to wield influence.

You must therefore do more than just understand how to set up your LinkedIn profile and pick the right photo. Yes, the technical aspects are important, but to utilize these tools properly and reap their full rewards, you need to be willing to open yourself up, allowing yourself to be vulnerable in a way you may not be used to. You need to take the time to understand and admit who you want to be as a leader and how your authentic self will engage your audience. As a leader, you already bring so much substance to social conversations, and a sense of knowledge of the bigger issues that others lack. You bring a lifetime of experience granting insight and guidance, and a deeper sense of what can move, affect, and lead your people.

You're not just out there talking about your product knowledge anymore either. Your teams, your customers, and your audience want to know how *you* feel about the issues at hand. They want to see how *you* represent the organization you run. They want the raw, uncut truth, not a prepackaged communications sales pitch. Previously, the leader's personal position was rarely taken into consideration, especially when dealing with social issues. That's no longer the case. Climate change, systemic racism, gun control, remote work, reopening schools, and reopening the economy, are all issues that require the attention of leaders today, and the personal opinions of these leaders play some of the key parts in how any company's message is told. It's no longer just, "here's a statement from the company," but who's stating it and why they are in a position of authority to talk about it. If you don't build that authority through these tools, you are no longer qualified to lead a twenty-first century organization.

All this work is part of running a financially successful business—it's about engaging with customers on a deeper level to actually help them improve their lives. It's about being a voice of stability and sanity among the noise and chaos out there. It's about making the world a better place by using your platform to enact change. Sure, a digital-first leadership culture within your organization is great, but what about the greater culture, one in which we can connect, collaborate, and come together beyond division and short-term thinking, and beyond the barriers that divide us? This may sound idealistic, but without idealism, and a bold approach, what's the point of leading anyone anywhere at all?

Though many of the principles throughout this book may feel overwhelming, just know you're not the only one who feels this way. I've worked with countless leaders who have only just begun to understand the importance of digital presence and the value of these tools. As they undertake this digital transformation, carving out their virtual real estate, I've been able to guide them along the way. But doing it on their own at first can be daunting; deciding on content, selecting the timing, and choosing specific wording can all be confusing tasks for beginners. Often, they only need thirty minutes of my time a week to set them on the right path. Most are simply looking for a mentor to help them get up to speed, develop the right habits, and build "muscle memory" so these tools become part of their regular routine.

After ninety days of help and guidance though, I'm usually able to turn my clients loose. Once they tell me they've got it, I know it's time to move on, which is always the plan—I'm here to assist, not to take over. No one can play your specific leadership role except you, and as an authentic digital-first leader, you'll be able to build the strength and reach of that role further. But you have to start somewhere. To begin, feel free to reach out to me, and let's discuss how we can collaborate together.

I'm easy to find—just look me up on LinkedIn.

ACKNOWLEDGMENTS

This multi-year project would not have been possible without the support and encouragement of a team of people. First is my wife, Stephanie, to whom this book is dedicated. She has been supportive, patient, and encouraging; words fail to describe her endless contributions. The hours of writing, rewriting, and persistence I was able to muster were all because I knew she was there for me, and I didn't want to let her down.

Additional thanks and acknowledgments:

To Jerry Chacon, who sat in my living room more than two years ago and talked me through the concept of bringing my ideas to the world through a book. His excitement for me to get started pushed me off the couch and to the keyboard.

To Tom Mendoza, whose friendship I have valued for many years as we navigated the new world of digital-first leadership. His willingness to continually put himself out there, to learn new things, and to allow me to be a coach and advisor helped me see how ideas can become action.

To Brian Bakstran, who reminded me on a regular basis that writing is hard, that writing a book is harder, and to never doubt that I can do it.

To Gail Mercer-MacKay, who continually reminded me that if I stayed with a dream and an idea long enough, it will come true.

To Peter McKay, who provided such great examples for how far and how fast an executive can adapt and change to the new world of digital-first leadership.

To Claire Pfeiffer, who stepped up as the project manager to push the book to the finish line.

To Zach Gajewski, whose expertise, professionalism, and incredible writing, meant he was able to take a year of content, condense, and organize it into the book you have in your hands.

To Rana Salman, PhD, who made our journey a shared one as we both discovered the new world of online presence.

To Scott Pfeiffer, because we have been through so much together, giving each other support to find our way to the promised land. For his unfailing optimism and keen insight about where the business world is going.

To David Blain, a friend and a confidant for more than 20 years, whose understanding of my story has always inspired me to trust my instincts.

To Mercedes Adams, whose trust and continued faith in me provided a deep well of support that I was able to draw upon.

To Maggie Bliss, who loves me and was willing to put up with me because I'm her father as I worked my way through the process.

And finally, to the BlissPoint team, who didn't exist before the project started, but who became a critical reason for the book to come to market. To Lorri Randle, Lia Bliss, Sheena Steedman, Jeff Stratford, Cammon Randle, and Marcie.

ABOUT THE AUTHOR

Richard Bliss is the founder of BlissPoint Consulting, a social media consulting company that helps improve executives' online communications and the social selling behaviors of sales teams. A LinkedIn Top Voices Influencer, experienced executive communications manager, and social media coach, he has helped thousands of people master social media tools and become fluent in social conversations, building their platforms and confidence to effectively reach their audience, define their brand vision and strategies, and develop high-caliber sales teams. In addition to working with businesses and organizations in the US, he's consulted startups and high-growth technology firms around the world.

A former executive vice president of marketing for eighteen years, and an award-winning pioneer in technology, collaboration, and cloud computing, Richard has appeared on CNN and other major media outlets. He shifted his attention to social media when he founded the podcast *Funding the Dream*, which became a leading voice in the crowdfunding space. Today, Richard continues to empower others through his weekly newsletter and podcast, which reach over 45,000 subscribers.

Richard lives in Silicon Valley where he juggles life between five daughters and setting world records playing board games. He can be found on LinkedIn at https://www.linkedin.com/in/bliss/.